THAT NATION MIGHT LIVE

A Story of Motherhood
Abraham Lincoln
The Civil War

One Afternoon with Lincoln's Stepmother

How true it is,
we can't stop loving
you anyway! Just
can't do it, *Jeff*

Jeff Oppenheimer

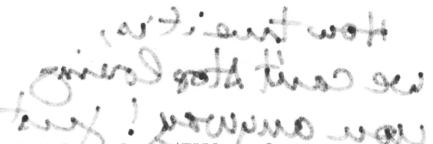

ISBN-13: 978-1497538771

Printed in the United States of America.

For Shellie

Table of Contents

Author's Note

On September 8, 1865, Abraham Lincoln's longtime friend and law partner, William H. Herndon, visited the martyred President's aged stepmother, Mrs. Sarah Bush Johnston Lincoln. Herndon's notes are integrated into the following fictional recreation of their afternoon together. The selected events in the life of Abraham Lincoln are real. The accounts are preferably first person. License was taken to convert these moments in the life of Lincoln into ten stories told from a rocking chair.

September 8, 1865

"When I first reached the home of Mrs. Lincoln and was introduced to her by Colonel A. H. Chapman, her grandson by marriage, I did not expect to get much out of her. She seemed so old and feeble ... She breathed badly at first but she seemed to be struggling at last to fix her mind on the subject. Gradually by introducing simple questions about her age, marriage, Kentucky, Thomas Lincoln, her former husband, her children, grandchildren ... [she] awoke, as it were, a new being. Her eyes were clear and calm; her flesh is white and pure, not coarse or material. She is tall, has bluish large gray eyes."

William H. Herndon,Esq.
Old Mrs. Lincoln's home,
Goosenest Prairie, Illinois

W. H. HERNDON.
A. ORENDORFF.

Springfield, Ill., September 8, 1865

Dearest Anna,

I cannot work. I cannot rest. My good friend is gone, yet is with us in Spirit. The news of his going struck me dumb, the deed being so informally wicked, so monstrous, so huge in consequences, that it is too large to enter my brain. Hence, it is incomprehensible, leaving a misty distant doubt of its truth. It is grievously sad to think of one so good, so kind, so loving, so honest, so manly, and so great, taken off by the bloody murderous hands of an assassin.

We exist now in the midst of two civilizations – one in the North and one in the South. The one will try and make Mr. Lincoln a perfect being, a supernatural man, and the other will say he is a devil; and so he will travel down all time misapprehended, not understood and, pray, whose fault will it be? The middle man is needed. Hence I have two things in view: first, sympathy for Lincoln, and, secondly, solidity for his memory. The recorded life sayings and doings of Lincoln will out-last all the artistic lives of Lincoln written during this age — Mark that.

The train takes me further from you still, yet under my finger, as if by some loving spell, I still feel the tip tap of baby's Nina's Blessed heart.

LAW OFFICE
OF
HERNDON & ORENDORFF,

W. H. HERNDON
A. ORENDORFF.

I feel her snuggled safe between us. These tender
moments are all a man can pray for, and God
has blessed me with His supreme joy. To have
life with you, Anna, is a gift perhaps unworthy
of this sloth; but a gift I bother not question,
accepting it only with the greatest joy. That
you, a woman of such wisdom, good humor,
and beauty, would agree to marry me, is proof
of Providence beyond the reach of the most
measured skeptic. And so it is, to be wrenched
from your side, Sweet Anna, is nothing sparing
anguishing sorrow. I forgo, as so many have
sacrificed long past awful misery that ~~we~~ that
nation might live.

The battle for Union has concluded. The battle
for Truth has commenced.

Would to God the world knew what I do, and
save me the necessity of being the man to open
and explain all. I am satisfied, in connection
with my own knowledge of Mr. L. for 30 years
that his whole early life remains to be written.
What made him so tender, so good, so honest, so
just, so noble, so pure, so exalted, so tolerant, so
divine?

This is my journey.

Your loving Husband,
Billy

All that I am,
or ever hope to be,
I owe to
my angel mother.

My Angel Mother

Old Mrs. Lincoln's home,
Goosenest Prairie, Illinois
Friday, September 8, 1865

I, William H. Herndon of Springfield, Illinois, hereby present the deposition of Sarah Bush Johnston Lincoln, the second wife of Thomas Lincoln, and stepmother of President Abraham Lincoln.

My railroad journey was twenty-seven hours and 100 miles to Mattoon Station. There I was greeted by Colonel Augustus H. Chapman at the Essex House. The impressive brick structure, combining hotel and rail depot as I have never seen before, sprung from the prairie like corn when the North/South Illinois Central intersected with the East/West Terre Haute Alton line.

Colonel Chapman steered his two-horse buggy to this cabin eight miles south, to the home of the President's aged stepmother. I recall from my approach across the open plain a shingled, pitched-roof, unpretentious building with a wide porch stretched across its front. Beside the door an ox yoke is hung there. Chapman said it is a tribute of sorts for Lincoln's father. Morning Glories climbed freely on it.

I dismounted on the horse path while Colonel Chapman made my presence known. I was soon greeted by Matilda Johnston Hall, the lone surviving child of Mrs. Lincoln. She led me into the right side door of the saddlebag cabin, comprised of two single room log cabins with separate entrances, connected by clapboards and a shared central chimney. Sword lilies came up plentifully alongside the footpath leading to Mrs. Lincoln's door, her residence for most of her adult life.

I stooped to clear the low doorframe. Firelight glinted off the dishes in the polished black walnut bureau sitting proudly beside the fire in the near corner.

Opening the door to the plains let in a gust that brightened the fire momentarily, revealing Mrs. Lincoln dozing in her rocking chair, clad neck-to-shoe tip in a black woolen dress. In a reclining position it is evident that Mrs. Lincoln is tall and lean. Her chair sits on an emerald green rag rug, an island on an oak floor scrubbed clean and glossy, smooth as still water.

Colonel Chapman leaned close to Mrs. Lincoln's rocking chair. Around her stooped shoulders was draped a woolen shawl. "Do you need another log on the fire, Granmarm?"

Summer still owned the plains so it was, to my surprise and discomfort, Mrs. Lincoln prolonged the fire even as the day approached noon. His words seemed to revive her. "Thank'ee, dearie," she murmured. "Don't mind a'tall." I removed my coat.

I was introduced to her by her daughter, Matilda Johnston Hall, known to all as Tildy. I did not expect to get much out of Mr. L's stepmother. She seemed so old and feeble. She breathed badly at first but she seemed to be struggling at last to fix her mind on the subject. Gradually by introducing simple questions about her age, marriage, Kentucky, Thomas Lincoln, her former husband, her children, grandchildren . . . she awoke, as it were, a new being.

Her flesh is white and pure, not coarse or material. She is tall, has bluish large gray eyes set deeply below level brows, framed by a scoop-shaped bonnet and softly curled gray hair. With visible strain she settled upon my countenance and slowly focused. "Where Mr. Lincoln once lived—his friends, too?" she asked.

"In Springfield, Illinois," I said once more. "I am William H. Herndon, his friend of thirty years and law partner of sixteen."

Muffled, and barely audible, she repeated her question, "Where Mr. Lincoln once lived—his friends, too?"

Mrs. Lincoln faded back into the fire's glow while Col. Chapman repeated his introductions, to which she seemed to have no apparent comprehension. I requested her to give me a sketch of her life, and stated that it might prove useful and interesting as a matter of history. After a protracted silence I spoke of her son as a man who was kind, tender and sympathetic, who felt deeply in the presence of suffering, pain, wrong, or oppression of any shape. He was the very essence and substance of truth—the exact truth—was of unbounded veracity, and had unlimited integrity. He was just to all, he loved the right, the good, and true, with all his soul. Mr. Lincoln expressed his great feelings in his thoughts and his great thoughts in his feelings. By these his soul was elevated and purified for his work.

She had no observable registration to my professions. As hope of any insights into my dearest friend began to fade, Mrs. Lincoln turned and looked upon my face. Her eyelids began to wrinkle and eventually lift and I saw again her bluish large gray eyes.

"I loved him also." She said no more.

Mrs. Lincoln sat up in her rocking chair and smoothed out her skirt with her snowy, slightly gnarled hands. A white linen bonnet, trimmed in lace, covered her gray hair and tied neatly beneath her chin. Her face is as peaceful as a newborn babe's when she dozes. Awake, she is alive with seemingly unspecified interest.

"Oh, yes." She nodded, leaning back in her rocking chair once again. "Where Mr. Lincoln once lived—his friends, too. And you say you were a friend of his?"

I spoke of her son as the best friend I ever had. He was the best friend I ever expect to have, and I repeated to her that I think Mr. Lincoln was the best man, the kindest, tenderest, noblest, loveliest, since Christ. Something I said roused her considerably. With a single, sustained breath she spoke:

"I've known since he come back from New Orleans that second time..."

I could not prompt her to provide additional account regarding said return from New Orleans. I began to return my quill to its case when Mrs. Lincoln stirred. She awoke new once more. Her clear eyes returned, Mrs. Thomas Lincoln Says —

"I knew Mr. Lincoln in Ky — I married Mr. Johnson — he died about 1817 or 18 — Mr. Lincoln came back to Ky, having lost his wife — Mr. Thos Lincoln and Myself were married in 1819 — left Ky — went to Indiana — moved there in a team. Here is our old Bible dated 1819: it has Abe's name in it. Here is Barclay's dictionary dated 1799: it has Abe's name in it, though in a better hand writing — both are boyish scrawls.

"My eyesight is good but I have trouble sometimes in threading a fine needle. I been better the past winter than common. My teeth are all gone, except two old snags. I am not much account any more, but I am still here mostly, or as much as I ever was. Want to know what kind of boy Abe was? Babies weren't as plenty as blackberries in the woods of Kaintuck. When I heard the news that Nancy Lincoln had her baby, I long to see her. Danny fussed about doing much of anything, so I hoisted my babe Betsy tight to my ribs and got to walking. You'd a thought he might come chasing after us, but not Daniel Johnston. My first husband was born tired.

"I made the trip down to Lincoln's farm on Nolan Creek where Nancy was recovering. Was near a mill owned by a man by name of Hodgens, had a spring on the claim, as I recall. I found Nancy there in the cabin, laying there in a pole bed looking purty happy. Tom'd built up a good fire and throwed a bear skin over the covers to keep them warm, and set their little two-year-old Sairy on the bed, to keep her off the dirt floor. Yes, there was only a dirt floor in the cabin.

"Lil Sairy and Betsy set there at the foot of the bed and stared at the new babe, point to him a bit, mostly tended to their corncob babies whilst Nancy and I tended to the infant. Yes sir, there were four mammies in that one-room cabin that night! Nancy had washed her little perfect babe and put a yellow flannel petticoat on him. He looked just like any other baby at first, like red cherry pulp squeezed dry.

"'What you going to name him, Nancy?' I asked her.

"'Abraham,' she says. 'After his grandfather that come out to Kaintuck with Daniel Boone. He was mighty smart and wasn't afraid of nothing, and that's what a man has to be out here to make anything out of himself.'

"Betsy and Sarah rolled up in a bear skin, slept by the fireplace that night, with a little corner for me so I could see the little feller when he cried. That was the first time I set eyes on Abe. I can scarcely say, even from his very first, he was mighty good company, solemn as a papoose, but interested in everything. Abe never was much for looks. Looks didn't count them days nohow. It was strength and work and daredevil. A lazy man or a coward was just poison, and a spindling feller had to stay in the settlements. The clearings hadn't no use for him.

"Tom had to git up and tend to his baby boy's needs at times, some a Nancy's too. Tom was kind and loving and kept his word, and always paid his way, and never turned a dog from the door. That's my second husband, and Abe's father. Dare say he's my last. Any more lost suitors might best turn right round!

"I was girl still first time Tom Lincoln shown his face in Liztown. (Writer – Elizabethtown, Kentucky) He come around for the work when we were building a mill. I confess I did not object to being at the center of a crowd. From my earliest recollections I known folks were prone to fawn on me. Sinful pride that was. I gussied myself up and brung one of my Mama's kittles to the stream so I could bring them working men water. Tommy Lincoln try to keep to himself, Mr. Herndon, but that was not to my liking so I pester him some. He was a young man then, vocal as a tree stump. Most natural that he did not object to my attention.

"I grown up Sally Bush - particular in my personal appearance, and in the selection of my gowns, and in the company I kept. I had long been accounted a proud body, holding my head above common folks. Some of my own kin felt the same. Never figured twice about it as I was living it. As I figured it, the decence of my dress and purt friends, stoked up envy. No surprise then some would hiss about it.

"Over the years Tommy Lincoln become real familiar to us Bushes. He was a Patroller for a while when my father was Captain. Seem like Tom was kin then. When I was young still, Tommy asked me to marry him. I was barely a woman, and Tommy was a full ten years older than I. Made my share a fool decisions. I did not marry Tom back then. Maybe Tommy Lincoln wasn't no challenge for me. Or the truth could be simpler still, and the truth might be I was sparking on a certain bushy haired Danny Johnston, the same one all the girls were whispering sin about when we supposed to be singing scripture at camp meetings on Green River Lake. And it wasn't too long afore that same Danny started sparking up sweet right back on me. He smelled like clean pine. I liked that, I liked it too much.

"Just round then, Tommy Lincoln picked up and took off with my own brother Isaac for New Orleans, only the Good Lord knew when they might return. They took by flatboat, pass through Cheyenne and Chickasaw country, didn't have fancy riverboats going up and down river back then. You know how they had to make their way home, Mr. Herndon? They walked!"

Mrs. Lincoln smiled broadly and I could see that the memory amused her greatly. Then, a shadow of concern clouded her features as she inquired, "I stray off topic, Mr. Herndon? My words'll sometimes follow my wandering mind like a baby fox to its crazy Mama."

"Please, Mrs. Lincoln, do not give it a thought," I assured her. "I am much obliged for the pleasure of your company, and interested in anything you have to say." I further explained that I hoped, in deposing her story as a matter of course, she would include any peculiarity or specialty of her stepson and his boyhood that she recalled.

"The examples you have provided already, I think, are excellent. It is all new to me." I went on to assure her that the information would be valuable in many ways and so it is best she speak freely. Mrs. Lincoln seemed content with my encouragement. I prompted her with a question about her first husband. She continued:

"I was determined to marry the Prince of our little circle, Mr. Daniel

Johnston. I was gonna be Sarah Bush Johnston, and I knew better than those plagued choruses of fool-calling I heard all around me. My own father refused to sign the marriage bond, making it known for all his feelings on the subject, so my brother Elijah signed by making his mark.

"Danny and I had our times, then children come along, first Betsy, then Tildy, and he still wasn't doing a stitch a work. Things weren't as charming to me then as they once were. Soon I was a squawking hen with a babe on each hip. I puzzle still how fast change come. Soon enough we owed so much money we found ourselves standing afore our neighbors on a delinquent list. Then Danny went and borrowed from my brothers and when he couldn't pay them back, they went to suing my husband and me for the notes. We were held as without funds. Mama laughed and laughed for my payback before she would cry and cry. My father seemed a tinge joyful to see me humbled before God as I was."

She blinked then, rapidly, I suspect to withhold tears. Mrs. Lincoln continued:

"My Pa knew nothing about a boy named Abe Lincoln. Nancy's boy was dutiful to me always—he loved me truly I think. I did not want Abe to run for President. I did not want him elected, was afraid somehow or other, felt it in my heart that something would happen to him; and when he came down to see me after he was elected President, I still felt that something would befall Abe and that I would see him no more. Abe and his father are in Heaven, I have no doubt, and I want to go there, go where they are. God bless Abraham."

Here the old lady stopped — turned around and cried — wiped her eyes — and proceeded:

"Tom married Nancy soon after Danny and me were married. Our lives were daily together one last time when we were both trying to make it in Liztown. Right round the same time Nancy and I have our first babes, and both girls. That's Sairy from Nancy, and Elizabeth was mine. We called her Betsy. She was a purt beauty from the git." Mrs. Lincoln stared into the flame, searching for answers. After a respectful pause I reminded Mrs. L. she was speaking of her life in Elizabethtown, KY, after she and Nancy had their baby girls. She resumed:

"Danny was doing a fine job spending Pappy's money like he was a nobleman, and Tommy's trying to work as a carpenter. It wasn't Tom's fault he couldn't make a living by his trade. There was scarcely any money in that country. Every man had to do his own tinkering and keep everlastingly at work to git enough to eat. So Tom took up some land further out, mighty ornery land. It was the best Tom could git, when he hadn't much to trade for it. Nancy moved off when Abe was in her belly. We had to move him to the side for a proper goodbye. Tom tried to farm stubborn ground and make a home from the timber he cut. It was rough living—the floor was packed dirt. The door swung on leather hinges. There was one small window and a stick-clay chimney. Poor Nancy! Next time we seen each other we laughed and laughed about how we were no longer girls, just before we cried and cried."

"I seen Tom and Nancy at gatherings or storing at Bleakey's. Seen Abe and Sairy too. Abe grown taller each time, skinny like a rail. He never give Nancy no trouble after he could walk, except to keep him in clothes. Most of the time he went b'arfoot. I heard Tommy and Nancy were having to stretch, and then I'd see Nancy and it'd seem to solidify the Lincolns were poorer than anybody. She's always a dignified personage, just roughed up from grubbing roots to feed her babes. And splitting rails and hunting and trapping didn't leave Tom no time to put a puncheon floor in his cabin, so they were living on dirt floors. It was all he could do to get his family enough to eat and to cover them.

"Nancy was powerful ashamed of the way they lived, but she know'd Tom Lincoln was always doing his best. She wasn't the pestering kind no how. She was purty as a picture and smart as you'd find them anywhere. She could read and write. Tom thought a heap of Nancy, and was as good to her as he know'd how. He didn't drink, or swear, or play cards, or fight; and them were drinking, cussing, quarrelsome days. Tom was kind to all, still could whip a bully if he had to. He just couldn't git ahead somehow.

"When Abe wasn't b'arfoot he was running round in buckskin moccasins and breeches, a tow-linen shirt and coonskin cap. Yes, that's the way we all dressed them days. We couldn't keep sheep from the wolves, and poor folks didn't have scarcely any flax except what they could git trading skins. The Lincolns weren't much better off than Injuns. Tom got a hold of a better farm after a while, further out still, but he couldn't get a clear title to it. So when Abe was eight years old, the Lincoln's lit out for Indiana.

"Tommy told me years later that Kaintuck was gittin stuck up, with some folks rich enough to own slaves, didn't seem no place for poor folks anymore. Might say too, Tommy was Separate Baptist, and he didn't care for profanity, intoxication, gossip, horse racing, or dancing - certainly did not care for slaving.

"'Every man must skin his own skunk,' Tom liked to say about those times.

"Indiana wasn't even a state yet when Tommy went up there to claim his land. Forest was as the Good Lord created it in the Beginning. Tommy said there were trees twenty foot round, and the forest floor was buried in grapevines to his waist, some stems he said were a full nine inches round. Abe told me once that there were hairy elephants that roam the same woods till the Injins killed them off. I think he was just fooling on me."

I informed Mrs. Lincoln that, in fact, the Wooly Mastodon evolved to survive cold climate, then had to migrate south due to the Ice Age. Evidence suggests big animal hunters crossed from Asia into North America over a land and ice bridge. Mrs. L. enjoyed this - said listening to me felt as though Abe had returned with his explanations. She continued:

"Tommy settled on land I was eventually to live on. And with all that land to choose from Mr. Herndon, would you know that my future husband selects a clearing for the salt-licks, and all his good hunting. Was over a fool mile from the nearest stream! No sir, I ain't much for picking them.

"I made sure to say goodbye when the Lincolns lit out for Indianny. Never seen Nancy Hanks Lincoln again. Everything they had worth taking was piled on the backs of two pack horses. Tom said to Nancy he could make new pole beds and puncheon tables and stools, easier than he could carry them. Said goodbye to the newborn they buried on Muldraugh's Hill. Climbed 400 feet up to the Little Mount Cemetery where a plot was marked by a limestone slab. Tom said he had to brush off the debris to reveal 'T.L.' chiseled into the surface of the stone. There lay his namesake, his baby boy who lived long enough to be given a name, though the poor lil feller wasn't to stay long enough to have his name inscribed in the family Bible."

Mrs. Lincoln dabs her tears dry with her handkerchief. Continues:

"Offin they went. Lincolns reached their new home about the time the state came into the Union. It was a wild region, with many bears and other wild animals still in the woods. There Abe grew up."

After some pause that appeared all Mrs. Lincoln was to speak on the subject. I inquired about the Bush family—her mother, father and her siblings, and how she had grown up.

"Well, Mr. Herndon . . ." She paused. "Some of my kin got rebel in them."

"Please do speak plainly, Mrs. Lincoln," I entreated. "My own father disinherited me, after calling me an 'abolitionist pup.' Come, now—be candid. Who was your father? What was he like?'" I encouraged her unrestrained comment. Mrs. Lincoln wrapped her shawl tighter about her shoulders before she continued:

"My father was Christopher Bush," she said, staring into the fire. "My father and brothers were known as stalwart men. There was no back-out in them. Never shunned a fight where they considered it necessary to engage in it, and nobody ever heard a Bush, my father or my brothers, cry, 'enough.'

"My brother Isaac once had a bullet extracted. He refused the doctors when they prepared to tie him down. He just lay down on a bench and placed a musket ball between his back teeth. Chewed it to pieces while the surgeons cut nine whole inches before they got the bullet. He didn't so much as wince when they removed it from his leg.

"My mamma was Hannah Bush. We were one of the first to settle in Kaintuck. My Pa went out with his family and his brother. Uncle wasn't made for the clearing and was scalped soon after we arrived. My Pa had my oldest brother, William, who was by then a man himself. Samuel and Hannah were still just chillern, and Isaac was a nursing babe. Eventually there were nine of us Bush children. My Pa built up all kinds of land. I got some of it, Mr. Herndon. My Pa was a generous man.

"Pa and my brothers were Patrollers. Tommy Lincoln was too. Pa was the Captain. Tommy couldn't do it for too long - couldn't stomach returning run-aways back South. My Pa and brothers didn't see it as such. The whipping posts were for all colors, so long as law was to be prop'ly respected."

Mrs. Lincoln stared back at me blankly. I inquired about the passing of her first husband, Daniel Johnston.

The old lady nodded and smiled and set her rocker to moving with a quiet, regular creak on the oak floor, seemed to reflect for a moment.

"It wasn't long after, Danny got himself appointed jailor for Hardin County. He was providing a roof over our heads, us Johnstons and the prisoners too. We were all under one roof. I raised my babes in stone jail set up, ancient-like, with prisoners living in cells beneath us. I born my last one in earshot of them prisoners. Can you imagine it? That was my boy, John D. 'D' was short for his father Daniel, through and through! It was not as I figured me when my sisters and I had our corncob babes back in the playing days. I cooked and cleaned for prisoners mostly, for Danny's job it was.

"Danny died soon after the Lincolns moved to Indiana. He couldn't hold any food down and eventually heaved himself to his last breath. Then Nancy died of milk-sick plague in Indiana. Nancy would a lived to be old if she'd had any kind of care, and I reckon she must a been strong to a stood what she did.

"Figuring the rest is easy enough, right up to Tom Lincoln showing up at my door with his speech prepared. History now, but on that day it was quite a thunderclap. Betsy was off schooling and I was knitting my wares while Tildy and John D. done their best not to poke the other in the eye. The door knocks and who you reckon is standing there, Mr. Herndon, but barrel-chested himself, Tommy Lincoln. He was quick about it, saying he had no wife and I had no husband. He says he came a purpose to marry me. He know'd me from a gal and I know'd him from a boy. He had no time to lose, he said, and if I was willing let it be done straight off.

"'Well,' I says, 'I can't do it.'" I let that set while Tommy turned whiter than the underbelly of fish. Needed to slow this charging bull some while I got my wits returning home between my ears.

I said to him I could not on account of my debts, and just like that he asked for the notes. Sure enough he comes back with my debts paid, and my assembled family was in agreement that Tommy was good folk. Afore I could even foster a second thought, I was marrying Tommy Lincoln and moving to the clearing across the Ohio River from my kin. Was so cold seem like the wolves ate the sheep just for their wool. Offin we went nohow.

"We crossed the Ohio at Thompson's Ferry, just opposite the mouth of the Anderson River in Indiana. That was a big entry point for the settlers that come through Kaintuck. The charges were prescribed by law about this time, and though times it feels I cannot remember my own name, I still recall it was a dollar for a horse and wagon, 25 cents for a man and horse, 12 ½ cents for great cattle, 12 ½ cents for foot passengers. Children were free.

"Didn't take long for John D. to start his squirming so I held on to his arm with white knuckles, and I'll never forget his face. I looked him square in the eye, said clear, 'John D, don't you go and lighten my load by falling off this boat into the Ohio River.' "He sat froze like he was plucked straight from a blizzard, Mr. Herndon!

The girls had eyes like pies. They ain't never been but a few miles from Liztown, and now they were crossing the Ohio with flatboats trailing one another like ducklings. Then we heard it afore we seen it, whistling right into the ear of the Lord, so loud. Was a side-winder steamer and them kids stretched in all directions, trying to see it all from their disappearing little world. I felt right then that I done them good.

"Was real relief on Tommy Lincoln, getting me across the river. Seemed to please him a great deal. Looking back I could see Negros loading their masters into a river skiff, but I just look forward, Mr. Herndon. And do you reckon what I saw, cause it was but one thing? Trees. Hundred-foot-high wall of trees.

"Abe told me later that he never passed through a harder experience than he did from Thompson's Ferry to the open-faced camp Tommy built on his claim. Tom may a showed Abe how to swing an axe back in Kaintuck, but the boy learned to use it right then to clear a path for the Lincolns to get through mostly thick brush. Called them roughs. Called 'em that for good reason.

"It was another three years afore Tommy brung me there. The roads weren't our trouble, it was the four horse wagon load of goods. I packed in a table, a set of chairs, a clothespress, chest a drawers, a flax wheel, soap kittle, cooking pots, an pewter dishes, lot a goods like bedclothes and kitchenware, feather pillers, homespun blankets an patchwork quilts that all made a heap a difference in a backwoods cabin. This is the bureau I took to Indiana in 1819 — cost $45 in Kaintuck (Mrs. L points to the bureau.) Between all of us and the property, there wasn't room to cuss a cat without getting fur in your mouth.

"Tommy done his share of fussing about it as we heaved and rocked, sometimes just to gain a few inches, iffin that. He got right sure we should unload a few trunks, to which I could only offer kind words for his effort to push on, and shine a smile at him. Eventually he got cured of the idea and give up. He waited a long time for my company! Was clear from the git that Nancy wasn't much for sassing back. Tommy wasn't quite sure what's to become of his old self! Was good fun, Mr. Herndon, having a man with Virginia decency.

"I once asked Tommy which of us, me or Nancy, he liked best. Tommy paused on that one a long time. Finally he took hold of my hand, looked straight on me, solemn as an owl. Said he looked on it like a man choosing between two horses: one that kicks and the other that bites. That's what Tommy done for me – kept my belly aching from his antics and yarns.

"Tommy said settlers called it Little Pigeon Creek for the abundance of the critters. I seen the upper branches start to wave sorta frantic like, then the sky turn dark from black clouds. Seem like a storm, 'ceptin for a squawking that might deafen us all were it to carry on much further. I never seen nothing like it back in Kaintuck. Come to figure what turn day to night was miles and miles of pigeons, far as I could see. The country was wild still, the panther's scream filled the night with fear. Ground hogs were snorting and squealing in the brush. Here I took my babes outta Liztown, the county seat, and we seen wolves, and a paw print that look like someone set a kittle right there in the river bank.

I slept with Tommy's rifle aside me, figuring if whatever made the paw print come along, this gun ain't gonna kill it, just gonna make it mad. I struggled all night figuring what to do, settling on nothing, just froze like, listening to the howling and screaming, and rustling from all directions. Tommy and the children were sleeping along like they were somehow protected.

"Sunrise wasn't much help. The forest turned from black to gray. Now I could see critters swarming instead of just hearing them. In gray daylight least I seen what was to eat me and my babes afore it happened. That was the comfort daybreak give me. Lord a-Mighty, what I done to my babes I was to fret. Tommy was funning the children with his yarns and such when sudden like he draw quiet as field mouse during Sunday sermon. Should a had some sense a trouble when he declare, quiet-like to me alone, that we were gittin close. I smelled it afore I seen it. Sheep and swine were running unpenned, their paws coated in mud and dung. I think to myself then, Nancy's babies!

"We come through snow and branches as we contended with a long and dreary winter. Finally seen the Lincoln cabin coming into sight. My chillern seen Sairy and Abe standing in front. They must a heard us coming along. Betsy asked if they were runaway slaves. Their skin was earthen and they were tattered and scared like. They were kin with wilderness.

MY ANGEL MOTHER

When father and mother married
he had children
and we went to live with him,
and she took the children
and mixed us all up together
like hasty pudding,
and has not known us apart since.

Hasty Pudding

"When we landed in Indiana, Mr. Lincoln had erected a good log cabin. Tolerably comfortable. The country was wild—and desolate.

"Tommy, Abe and Denny (Writer clarifies - 'Denny' is Lincoln's cousin, Dennis Hanks. Lineal connection unclear. Married Sarah Bush Lincoln's oldest daughter - Betsy.) Them boys had already cleared a field for planting come spring. I seen charred tree stumps strewn about the winding rows. Considered the amount of food we'd coax out of it—peas, corn, carrots, potatoes and onions. I figured we would do right fine.

"Abe was then young, so was his Sister. He was about nine years of age and Sairy was about eleven. Tom told me on the road that she'd been grieving for Nancy and had purt near cried herself dry long afore he left to come and get me. My heart hurt for her. Couldn't get through them trees slower it seem then, I was fixin to git to Nancy's babes the more Tommy speak on them.

"It was December and cruel winds whipped through the trees. As we drew closer, I could see that Abe's hands were blue with cold. He was so thin, like a skeleton, and his frayed deerskin pants barely covered his knees. Both young'uns were filthy and wrung out, so dirty they looked dark skinned. Abe was nothing but a peculiar-looking skeleton—wild, ragged and dirty, but without the emptiness in his eyes the way his sister done.

"Might a buried Sairy right alongside her Mama had much more time gone by. May a been fitting as it goes. Sairy was Nancy's little shadow, choring buckets soon as she was upright, and keeping each other good company generally. Any time I seen them in Liztown Sairy was about hitched to Nancy's knee. They were sisters like, same brown hair and dark skin with similar blueish green eyes, similar in the face too, sharp and angular, each with a prominent forehead. Purt beauties! So sudden like that, Nancy's gone and poor Sairy is alone in the wilderness.

"Tom wasn't worth shucks then, says them that were there. Without Nancy, I spect he might not a held up. Abe and Denny try their best to cheer on Sairy. They brung her baby fawns and raccoons but she'd just set by the fire and cry. She's fragile as a goose's egg at that tender age nohow, and her whole connection to this world was Nancy - intellygent, and Godly, and tender Nancy.

"When she lay dying, Nancy seen the trials that'd come to her baby girl with no mama to guide and love her. Certainly strained her heart, but put nary a scratch on her love of the Lord. Nancy accepted her leaving Abe, Sairy, and Tom as the Will of the Father. Predetermined as such, she went with the trust of a child. She was Separate Baptist, some called them Hard Shell Baptist. Her faith was unbending—but I know'd her heart wasn't hard, not a bit."

Here the old lady stopped and turned in her chair as if to hide her tears. After a moment, she wiped her eyes, turned back to me and proceeded with her story:

"Sairy clung to me something awful. Abe wasn't so quick to it. Tommy commanded him to make his greetings to me, which Abe done and not much else. Called me 'Mam,' saying it low enough so Tom took no notice. Abe kept appearing from nowhere in particular, as I was seeking this and that. After I pushed aside the flapping bearskin Tommy satisfied himself was a doorway, I was across the packed dirt floor to clear the fire. It was dead of winter and they got no fire going. Them chillern were shivering with cold!

"I set aside the kittles that were sloshing with boiled squirrels. From the looks of it, smell of it too, might say it been there a day or so. Seemed like a few seasons of ashes had built up under the kittle. I turn around and there was Abe, hair swarming with lice, bony elbows and knobby knees sticking out everwhere. He was holding my birch twig broom and an old ash box, which he gave to me, and then he swooped that squirrel kittle away afore I could shine on him. Quick as a wink he was gone from my sight.

"I was fixin to fetch kindling when I about run into Abe. He was standing aside me with a heap of it in his long arms. His mind and mine, what little I had, seemed to run together, move in the same channel. He was measuring everything I done, and he was measuring it just right, kindly, otherwise kept to his business. Not so much as field mouse squeak from him. His eyes were mostly looking at the ground under his feet and they were were so black they seemed to disappear into the dirt floor. Abe's eyes were deeply hollowed into his skull, separated, you might say, with some authority, by his nose. His ears protruded from his head like apple wedges. I must say, Mr. Herndon, that boy was the most peculiar thing that ever obstructed my view."

Mrs. Lincoln amused, until her eyelids drifted downward. Just as I was sure she had fallen asleep, she roused herself and continued:

"I took pains not to appear hurried or worried none but inside I couldn't move quick enough to get them poor babes cleaned up and feeling human again. While I got the fire going strong, I give the chillern buckets and send them to the stream for water—a fool mile away! When they were gone, I set the washstand and basin and a gourd of soap outside, near the cabin opening. Fetched my soap kittle and another gourd to dip water with, and I eventually soaped and scrubbed until Abe and Sairy looked again as their good mother left them.

"I dressed Abe and his sister up with things I just pulled from my trunks until they begun looking a deal better. For little Sairy, it was as simple as reaching for one of Betsy's dresses. I plucked a bright blue calico that I figured would provide right nice contrast for Sairy's dark features. I just had to let out the hem a little. Them Lincolns were made long! Washed and cleaned as she was, she looked no relation to that half-starved creature I'd found. She screamed bloody murder when I brushed them thick scrobbles out of her hair. It brought me back just then to brushing Nancy's hair, whooping it up like girls who don't know better when there's no grown folks to reign us in. Sairy looked right beautiful again, just like her Mama. I pray right then for Peace for Nancy, wishing to let her know I was here now, and she don't need to worry about her babies any more.

"For Abe I had to sort through my first husband Danny's old wares. I had to cuff up the trousers some, but not much—the boy was taller than many men I seen, though he was still just boy compared to Danny. Shirt needed a bit more tapering so as not to hang like it was out to dry. Abe was so skinny he might a slipped through a pin hole!

"Abe was clean and dressed when an idea occurred to my fool head, just right then, and I went for my case and reached in for my mirror. I spun it round and handed it to the boy.

"Well, sir—he stared in it for naught but a wink and his voice, mostly unheard by me, come out clear as a church bell right then.

"'Land a Goshen, is that me?'

"Mr. Herndon, I swear, that flapping bearskin door come in handy right then. I figure if Tommy'd had a real door, that one-room cabin could not a held all the grinning we done just then, like eejits we were over it."

Here, the old lady stopped—amused and winded. After a few moments she is able to continue:

"Abe's bed was a pile of dry leaves laid in one corner of the loft. The roof dripped some. He climbed up to it by means of a series of pegs driven into the wall as a ladder, instead of stairs. The bedsteads on the main floor were original creations, made of poles fitted into holes bored in the logs of the cabin walls and supported inside by stakes driven into the dirt floor. My new husband was a carpenter by trade and ain't so much as made a puncheon floor or cabinet for his home. Had the best tools as any man fifty miles round, and he done the best carpentry work for others, fancy inlays and such—but under his own roof he lived on dirt floors. His table and chairs were slabs of clapboard with holes bored in the corners for the legs. Some say Tommy was shiftless. Maybe so, but I got me one this second time around, in Tommy, that I could fix up. Danny couldn't be mended nohow.

"Abe, Denny and John D. slept upstairs in the loft. I swept the piles of leaves away and give them boys proper beds and kivers, enough to keep them warm no less. The girls slept on my bearskin by the fire. Little Sairy just chirked right up with a mother and two sisters for company.

"Next morning Tom spoke it all on his own, saying he'd get started on lumber for a new floor. Tommy, Denny and Abe were getting dressed to fell trees, and though he didn't remark on it, I could tell Abe was right proud of his new clothes, even though they were only hand-me-downs.

"Abe asked my Johnny why he wasn't dressing too. Well it was Johnny's turn—he just chirked right up. Figure he ain't had no Pa for two years now, just two older sisters and his Mama. I was plumb worried the boy might develop buds, breathing the same air as all us girls as much as he was. Johnny got his winters on right quick. 'Best get enough for a proper bed for the three girls,' I told them.

"Abe, Tommy and Denny walked along into the woods with axes on their shoulders, little John hopping alongside. They gave him a branch hacksaw, which he swung freely. A wonder to me that men don't lose more limbs.

"That left us womenfolk free a men to get the cabin properly settled. First thing we done is move the table. I'd brung a hickory table and set of real chairs, not the three legged puncheon stools them poor Lincolns were setting on afore we arrived. I filled it up that little cabin with dishes, proper utensils, and feather beds and pillers, quilts and homespun blankets. I'd brung crate after crate of housewares and home goods from the wagon that could make a frontier cabin ever so much more comfortable, and I meant to use it all. This here black walnut bureau was a wedding present from all my many brothers and sisters, for me an Danny, living the high life with a $45 bureau.

"Tom and the boys brought back enough lumber to build beds for the chillern and make the floor for the cabin. That second night we settled in and Tommy led us in prayers and then we ate in tuckered out silence. First good meal those children had had since Nancy died, and I know they must a ben glad to be done with boiled squirrels. Afore we gone our ways I ask for clasped hands, and there wasn't any resistance among any of them. Maybe they were too warn thin to resist anything just then!

Back in my stuck-up days in Liztown, my Mama forced me to pray, but no matter how many times I repeated her prayer, nothing much changed. It stuck with me like a scar at first, finally just stuck with me. She seen me learn it from hard living before she passed to the Lord's loving arms.

"We gathered round. I made sure not to reach for Abe, so it was quite a sight to see his hand reaching for mine. We were clung tight, Mr. Herndon. So I says my Mama's prayer just then, with Abe's hand grasping my hand, and I couldn't a clung to him tighter if he was a babe dangling over a rough river:

> *He prayeth best who loveth best*
> *All things both great and small;*
> *For the dear God that loveth us,*
> *He made and loveth all."*

"It wasn't long afore Tom had a floor put in and whipsawed and planed off so I could scour it. We cleaned up the cabin nice, and chink the ceiling so it no longer drip on them boys while they slept."

Here the old lady rocked in her chair briefly before dozing off to sleep. On the table beside her are four books she brought from Kentucky. With Chapman's permission, I seized the opportunity to peruse their contents. They were: Robinson Crusoe, The Arabian Nights, Webster's Speller and Lessons in Elocution by William Scott. After review Writer concludes excerpts of Scott's text worthy of transcription:

Inscribed in the title page are the words, "Purchased by Isaac Bush at Bleakley and Montgomery store in Elizabethtown, Kaintuck. May 27, 1806." Page 36 "Eight requirements for a Polished Speaker:"

1. Let your articulation be Distinct and Deliberate.
2. Let your pronunciation be Bold and Forcible.
3. Acquire a compass and variety in the Height of your voice.
4. Pronounce your words with propriety and elegance.
5. Pronounce every word consisting of more than one syllable with its proper accent.
6. In every Sentence distinguish the more significant words by a natural, forcible and varied emphasis.
7. Acquire a just variety of Pause and Cadence.
8. Accompany the Emotions and Passions which your words express by correspondent tone, looks, and gestures.

Pages 55-91 were devoted to "Elements of Gesture," including drawings showing the correct positions of the body in speaking, with special attention to the hands and feet when gesturing. The remainder of the volume is devoted to "Lessons in Reading," beginning with, "Select Sentences." Examples Given:

"You must love learning, if you would possess it." KNOX
"Whatever you pursue, be emulous to excel." BLAIR

Following these pithy sayings are selections from the world's great literature, a treasure trove of readings, and likely Mr. L's introduction to Shakespeare, a lifelong love for him.

Sarah awoke refreshed and rejuvenated, and inquired what I held in my hands.

"These books were Mr. Lincoln's, were they not?" I asked, and when she nodded, I added, "He loved reading, did he not?"

"Oh, he did, indeed. Abe didn't like physical labor but was diligent for knowledge. Seem like he wanted to know everything about everything and I used to tell Tom if pains and labor would get it, then Abe was sure to get it. He read all the books he could lay his hands on. I can't remember dates nor names, I am about seventy-five years of age. Abe read the Bible some, though not as much as has been said. He sought more congenial books, suitable for his age.

"Nancy taught Abe how to read and write. Folks from miles around knew he was powerful smart. He'd write letters for people when he wasn't but eight. That was all Nancy's teaching. I didn't have no education myself, but I know'd what learning could do for folks.

"I wasn't in Indiana very long afore I found out how Abe hankered after books. 'Mama'—which he eventually got round to calling me—'Mama,' he'd say, 'the things I want to know is in books. My best friend's the man who'll git me one.' Well, books wasn't as plenty as wildcats, but I got him a few—had them in one of them trunks Tommy wanted me to leave in the wilderness to rot when we were journeying to the Lincoln homestead. I had one book that had a lot of yarns in it. One I recollect was about a feller that got near some darned fool rocks that drawed all the nails out of his boat and he got a duckin'. Wasn't a blamed bit of sense in that yarn. Well, I reckon, but I ain't no scholar.

"Abe'd lay on his stomach by the fire and read out loud. We'd laugh, though I reckon it went in at one ear and out at the other most times. Tom'd come in and say, 'See here, Abe. Your mammy kain't work with you a bothering her like that.' But I always said it didn't bother me none, and I'd tell Abe to go on. I reckon that encouraged Abe a heap.

"Denny says many a time, 'Abe, them yarns is all lies.'"

"'Mighty darned good lies,' Abe'd say right back, and go on reading and a chuckling to himself, up til Tom'd kiver up the fire for the night and shoo him off to bed.

"I reckon Abe read that Robinson Crusoe book a dozen times, and know'd them yarns by heart. We'd git hold of a newspaper once in a while, and Abe'd learn Henry Clay's speeches. He liked the stories in the Bible, too, and he got a little book of fables somewheres. I reckon it was them stories he read that give him so many yarns to tell. I asked him once after he'd gone to lawing iffin he could make a jury laugh or cry by firing a yarn at them.

"'Mama,' says Abe, 'when a story learns you a good lesson, it's more than a yarn. God tells truths in parables. They're easier for common folks to understand and recollect.' His stories were like that. If a man'd been doing anything low down, Abe'd make him feel meaner than a suck-egg dog about it.

"Seems to me now I never seen Abe, after he was twelve, that he didn't have a book somewheres around. He'd put a book inside his shirt and fill his pants pockets with corn dodgers, and go off to plow or hoe. When noon come he'd set down under a tree, and read and eat. When he come to the house at night, he would tilt a chair back by the chimney, put his feet on the rung, and set on his backbone and read. I always put a candle on the mantelpiece for him, if I had one. And like as not, Abe would eat his supper there, taking anything I'd give him that he could gnaw at and read at the same time.

"I've seen many a feller come in and look at him, Abe not knowing anybody was around, and sneak out again like a cat, and say, 'Well, I'll be darned!' It didn't seem natural, no how, to see a feller read like that. I never let the chillern pester him. I always said Abe was going to be a great man some day and I wasn't going to have him hindered."

Colonel Chapman came in then, to help Mrs. Lincoln to the table. "Mr. Herndon, we'd be pleased to have you take the midday meal with us."

"And I am most honored to accept your kind invitation, sir."

Sarah rose and took Col. Chapman's arm. I followed them through a narrow corridor that connected the two cabins. After a few steps with assistance Sarah walked on her own.

Standing nearly six feet tall, her frame unbent by time and her posture upright, her steps were sure and steady as we walked into the kitchen where her daughter Tildy was preparing. The room was brightened by the flame fully engulfing the bubbling kettle of blessed sustenance. At the center of the square single cabin was a circular table - set round with five places.

"I hope you will enjoy simple country fare, Mr. Herndon," Tildy welcomed me with a smile.

"It smells delicious," I observed. "What is in it that makes so tantalizing an aroma?"

She blushed modestly but was quick to offer, "Venison, Mr. Herndon, Denny shoot it fresh just yesterday. I cook it with a bit of ham and a few herbs from the garden. My Mama taught me long ago about layering the pot with the meat on the bottom and the herbs and taters and carrots on top, let all them flavor seep through." Mrs. Lincoln seemed charmed at the compliment, and a tinge tearful. Tildy invited us to take our places at the table.

Sarah was seated on my left. She asked if I would like her to repeat the prayer Tommy led before the Lincolns would gather for a meal. I enthusiastically agreed to her suggestion. Hands clasped, we said it in unison:

"Fit and prepare us for humble service, for the sake of Christ."

Ate dinner with her—sat on my west side—left arm—ate a good hearty dinner she did—stared at the kettle in silence. Mrs. Lincoln began again:

"First sign of spring, most a the settlers on Pigeon Creek was flocking to the giant kittles. The maple sap began to run and it was a good excuse for gathering after winter. Sugar camp we call it. Was a big event, it was then. Boys and girls had an excuse to sit together at night. Troubles run off from there. We kept the fire burning steadily and when the sap was boiled down, the stock was molded into hearts and stored in great jars.

"The men were off with jars a their own. Jugs with names like Black Betty got passed around plenty. Tommy would stay clear, being Hard Shell Baptist. Whiskey loosens jaws and plenty quick the men were yippin, all afire about this new state coming in, calling it Missouri. Was it coming in a Slaving state like Kaintuck, or Free as Indiana? Most of them men were Kaintuck like Tommy and me, living in Pigeon Creek to git away from slaving. The cheap government land titles were a draw too, Tommy say. But he couldn't git ahead nohow in Kaintuck, bidding against slave labor. There wasn't one thing Tommy liked about slaving, not in Kaintuck, Indiana, or this new Missouri.

"I was pleased as warm spice for the distraction of them men crowing back and forth. Men caw out for fools to hear. Them women were more like serpents - whispering serpents. I heard the hiss that Nancy ain't yet cold, and here Tommy been married again. They couldn't much know me so I took their words to mean they missed Nancy, figure we were more alike than they knew. Foolish to poke around a skunk, living to spray that stink as they are.

"Before long Tom had built me a loom, and when I heard of some lime burners being round Gentryville, I made Tom mosey on over and git some lime, and whitewash the cabin. And he made me an ash hopper for lye, and a chicken house nothing could git into. He put in a real door, cut out a window we filled with glass pane - I wouldn't stand for no such oilpaper as Tommy thought we should. He patched the crumbling from the stick-n-mud chimney and made the oak floor smooth as glass. With the door fixed the warmth stayed in while soft comfort was plenty available. Downstairs was two plump feather beads in the corners, piled high with warm quilts I'd made back in Liztown. The loft didn't get much of the heat from the fire, so the boys were most comforted by warm bedclothes. My kitchenware was plentiful around the clean fireplace, the dishes were clean and stacked on my $45 black walnut bureau.

"There were eight of us then to do for. Purty soon we had the best house in the country. There was no school that winter in Pigeon Creek as there weren't enough children. We got all fixed up soon enough and the children had time on end to enjoy the forest. Tommy and me made an easy peace. He was darn tickled to have me for a wife, and listening to me clearly done him some good, so we set out to get to know one another while the chillern were freed up with a blessed wilderness.

"Abe showed my young'uns how they could eat fox grapes right off the hanging vines. Then Betsy and Tildy showed Abe and Sairy how the kids in Liztown were using the ropes for funning. They cut down some vine and give one end to Abe and the other to John D. and had them swing it around so it was steady in rhythm, then they figure till the time was just right and jump right under it, and when it come round again they'd jump over it, and then just as soon, under it. They done that a plenty until they would find something else. Abe showed them how to make hoops using hickory saplings and rawhide, and so they went on, clowning along the day. Life was huckleberry pie.

I am going away from you, Abraham,
and shall not return.
I know that you will be a good boy;
that you will be kind
to your Sister and Father.
I want you to live as I have taught you,
and love your Heavenly Father.

3

Live as I have Taught You

"Deaf and blind to the movements of others, we were surrounded by the tallest trees of the Good Lord's creation. Folks were settling closer as time gone on. The Brooner family was half mile away. Still wilderness, but the men didn't have to wait for Gentry's store to get to jawing about Missouri coming into the Union. Alabama coming in Slave made it same number as the Free states. Missouri being Slave would mean we just as quick have more Slave than Free states. Most in Indiana was up in arms about it. So we brung in Maine as Free, and we were all even again. It was the year 1820 when them men finally quit their yippin about it.

"Abe, when old folks spoke, was a silent and attentive observer, never speaking or asking questions til they were gone and then he must understand everything, even to the smallest thing, minutely and exactly. He would then repeat it over to himself again and again, sometimes in one form and then in another; and when it was fixed in his mind to suit him he became easy, and he never lost that fact or his understanding of it. Sometimes he seemed pestered to give expression to his ideas and got mad, almost, at one who couldn't explain plainly what he wanted to convey.

"As company would come to our house, Abe would sometimes take a book and retire aloft, or go to the stable or field or woods and read. Abe was always fond of fun, sport, wit and jokes. He was sometimes very witty indeed. He never drank whiskey or other strong drink. He was temperate in all things, too much so I thought.

"Abe never told me a lie in his life, never evaded, never equivocated, and never dodged nor turned a corner to avoid any chastisement or other responsibility; was honest as they come. He never swore or used profane language in my presence nor in others that I now remember of, and he duly reverenced old age though he loved those best about his own age. But he played with those younger than him.

He listened to those older and argued with his equals. Abe loved animals, generly, and treated them kindly. He loved children well, very well. He treated everybody and everything kindly and humanely, though he didn't care much for crowds of people; he chose his own company which was always good.

"Time pass on and we got our routines and it wasn't too long afore we felt like the eight of us had never been apart. On the clearing was nothing but chores and family.

"When Denny was say twenty years old and Betsy was fifteen and then some, she come round asking my opinion if they were to marry. Wasn't no stopping it, my pestering would be about as discouraging on Betsy as my Ma's and Pa's was on me. Tommy said we'd just ask in a few in particular and do it soon. I plague him a bit on his new habit of proposing quick weddings. I figure what Tommy was having to say, which was, we were poor.

"About that time harvest was still a ways yet, there were eight of us to feed. Ate mostly game. Was a time when Tommy led the family in blessing the meal we were about to eat. All we had in front of us a few boiled taters as the fellers weren't too apt or lazy to bag us game. Quiet settled all round when Abe squeak out:

"Mighty poor blessings."

"Tommy might a cuffed him good had it not been for all the other chillern grinning like eejits. Abe was right of course.

"I sent Abe with a jug to a certain distiller, being there were expectations for a wedding, even if Tommy didn't partake. Got us a date with a preacher, and a short guest list, maybe fifteen in all. Denny went back to Kaintuck to fetch his half brother, John Hall. He must a gone hopping and skipping across the Ohio, thrilled by marrying my baby girl. Seem early to me but no point in figuring once young'uns get it in their heart. On the clearing there ain't much but chores and family. Best git them married off afore things become shameful. Wasn't no need for that.

"Denny come back from Kaintuck with John Hall, and the Preacher done it at noon that day. Betsy was flush in the cheeks like a young bride should be. Denny was goodness to the core, iffin a little peculiar and prone to speeching. Betsy could a done as poorly as her Mama done first time around, but she done OK with Denny. After the ceremony they sat by themselves in a corner, Betsy seeing nothing but Denny, and Denny looking like a cat that swallowed a bird.

"It begun to peck at Abe it seem, gittin to feel so much normal all of us together as family. He was not quite as upright. I see him try to fun his way out of this empty well. He'd get to firing his yarns, and he'd a scratch his arm with excitement as he'd get going. It would work for a little while. I resolved to stay a hawk above my far-eyed boy.

"We'd sit for evenings and hardly say but a word. Abe would read mostly, sitting on the floor folding his long form into the darnedest positions I ever seen. Times where he'd come and set next to me just as you and I are, right now. We ain't said but a word or two, and it comfort him I think, for me to set with him and not ask nothing of him. Speaking wasn't always necessary, the two of us. His mind and mine, what little I had, seemed to run together, move in the same channel."

"Abe begun to disappear now and again. I spy him closely, speak nothing of it. Only way to outfox a fox, Mr. Herndon... One day I took the horse path to the first fork and then circled back to a special knoll. Just as I figured, there was Abe. Was a field of graves, mostly unmarked. Abe lay there, lay where Nancy was buried. I come back to the cabin and let him be.

"One day I excused myself just as he was fixin to go. I went to Nancy's grave. Time come long when I heard Abe rustling through the trees and just hold up all at once. Paying him no mind, I prayed for Nancy while he stayed hidden. We done that once or twice more. Finally Abe come down to see me as I knelt at Nancy's grave. By the time he reached me, he'd been carrying his hurt heart for so long and I could see he was done hauling it. I pulled him to me and told him how much I missed his Ma. Abe was all boy for the first time for me, just then. I made sure to hold him up tight so he didn't have to carry that weight alone no more, and he let go.

"Abe told me the story, said how the cows started stumbling and struggling something awful just to brace themselves, and how their heads drop, knees lock, and then the trembling begins. Milk-sick plague come on. Was a pizon (Writer clarifies—poison) the cows were taking into their udders from grubbing on a root in the shade. Come to find out that it was drought that brought milksick. Herds were driven to the trees and the grass was dry, so they chewed on the roots for their moisture. Some roots run with the poison. The sight of a cow trembling was the shadow of death, and that begun the most God awful time which I ought not think on. Poor Nancy!

"Wasn't a doctor nearer than thirty-five miles. They didn't have no answers nohow, except for whiskey mostly, or baking soda. It wasn't no use. Pray for mercy, that's all. Whole families were laid to the ground in a week's times, dragging around like skeletons, afore they succumb. Nancy's own parents, Tom and Betsy Sparrow, were the first to pass. Those that were living tried boarding up their houses, or just moved off, but it done them no good. We were all just waiting for that darnded plague to move along and git.

"When it come, it begun with vomiting mostly, and then it was suffering one horror to the next, the tongue gets black as night, screaming belly pain, and blocked up every which way. The Brooners were the closest thing the Lincolns had for neighbors. Abe and the Brooner's boy... Henry was the Brooner boy's name. Abe and Henry were at times inseparable, and insufferable. Abe and Henry once walked to Vincennes, a distance of more than fifty miles, and while there they purchased a rifle gun in partnership for fifteen dollars. Times I wanted to turn it on both of them, but boys will be boys, and that's OK I reckon. When we moved to Illinois Henry purchased Abe's interest in the gun.

"Lord above, I'm fixin to talk you down all sorts of wilderness trails Mr. Herndon, seeing as what come next was plain awful. Plague was all around the Lincolns when Mrs. Brooner begun vomiting. Nancy Hanks done as Nancy Hanks done, and she went to her neighbor and cared for her, just as she done for her Ma and Pa.

"When Nancy came to tend to her, Mrs. Brooner said, 'I believe I will have to die.' Nancy was encouraging her not to give up hope and said, 'Oh, you may outlive me.' And Mr. Herndon, don't you know they were both gone but ten days later. Maybe Nancy put herself at risk tending to her neighbor, but that's what Angels do, and that's what Nancy was. Her heart couldn't stand it no other way.

"Nancy knew what was coming for her, having treated her Ma and Pa, and Mrs. Brooner. She know'd how it worked by then, so she called Abe and Sairy to her bed one at a time. Her words were calming and measured, just as Nancy was. Abe told me many a time, she said, 'I am going away from you, Abraham, and I shall not return. I know that you will be a good boy; and that you will be kind to your sister and father. I want you to live as I have taught you, to love your Heavenly Father and keep His commandments.'

"Tommy made those her last words to the chillern, keeping Abe and Sairy busy choring while they lived with Dennis, who was grieving over his parents too. Denny's parents, Tom and Betsy Sparrow, they were Abe's Granmarm and Grandpappy. Abe thought them blood kin till much later in his life. He never forgot the misery in that little green-log cabin in the woods when his Gram and

Grandpappy died, then come his Ma. Few things tax a heart greater in this world than a babe without a Mama, just as innocent as the Good Lord creates. Easy pickens too.

"Abe said how he helped Tom make the coffin. He took a log left over from building the cabin, and helped Tommy whipsaw it into planks and plane them. Abe held the planks while Tom bored holes and put them together with pegs Abe'd sat and whittled. There weren't scarcely any nails in the country and little iron, except in knives and guns and cooking pots. Appears to me like Tom was always making a coffin for someone.

"They laid Nancy close to the deer run in the woods. Deer were the only wild critters women weren't afraid of. Abe was somewheres round nine years old, but he never got over the miserable way his mother died. I reckon she didn't have no sort of care—poor Nancy! She was taken on a sled to the graveyard. Abe and Sairy rode the horse hitched to the sled. Abe remembered the driver was Old Man Howell, and that the man's long beard bothered him.

When Mrs. Lincoln's grave was filled, Mrs. Brooner's husband, Pete, extended his hand to Tommy and said, 'We are brothers, now.'"

While Mrs. Lincoln rests, Writer reflects on Nancy Hanks Lincoln:

The poor woman sleeping under the winter's snow had done her work in this world. Stoop-shouldered, sad—at times miserable—groping through the perplexities of life, without any prospect for the betterment of her condition, Nancy Hanks Lincoln passed from this earth, little dreaming of the grand future that lay in store for the ragged, hapless little boy who stood at her bedside the last days of her life.

Amid the miserable surroundings of a home in the wilderness Nancy Hanks passed across the dark river, God bless her. If I could breathe life into her again, I would do it. If only I could whisper in her ear, "Your son was President of the United States of America from 1861 to 1865," I would be satisfied.

I have heard much of this blessed Nancy Hanks Lincoln from Mr. L. Though of lowly birth and the victim of poverty and hard usage, she takes a place in history as the mother of a son who liberated a race of men. At her side stands another Mother whose son performed a similar service for all mankind eighteen hundred years before. God selects unpromising cradles for his greatest and best servants. At his Will and Tender Mercy, this very woman resting before me will stand among them, the sprightly woman who knew what education could do for people.

William H. Herndon, Sept, 1865 (Writer requires refreshment, retires).

The respite does my mind and hand good. Mrs. Lincoln mumbled unitelligably about Nancy as she rose to consciousness; her present mind able to resume what was begun, or continued, in dream state. "Nancy Hanks was base born," she spilled out clear enough. She continued:

"She told me herself once. Her Pa was from Virginny, a well-bred man, and he loved Nancy's Ma, but he did not live up to his commitments and Lucy Hanks was left with a baby that become the talk of the Shenandoah Valley. Hanks family had to pick up and git. Went West a course, to Kaintuck. Crossed through the Cumberland Gap as most done.

"I was born on the clearing, Mr. Herndon, never stepped a foot in any kind of a civilized Virginny. Lucy Hanks come from there with baby Nancy on her bosom. Soon after they arrive in Kaintuck, Lucy give baby Nancy up to her parents and just cut loose of her moorings. Taken enough shaming that she just set free. Wasn't long after she was brought afore the judge, on a charge that a lady does not speak of."

Mrs. Lincoln whispers her story to Tildy, who relays to Writer that Lucy Hanks was charged with fornication.

"Lucy's Pa wasn't for the clearing, he up and died. Lucy's Ma wasn't for the clearing as a widow, so she up and return to civilized Virginny. She went home alone, so Nancy was given up again. Lucy wasn't for taking her babe back. She was all new. A good man - distinguished like, come a courting Lucy Hanks. She was broken like a wild horse, and settle in for six children with this man who's name I can't recollect. No mind, Lucy taught all them six young'uns to read and write, and she died a real woman of society. She was there when Nancy married Tommy. When I come across her she was kindly, and civilized. Never could tell by watching her that day she was there at her babe's wedding pretending to be her Aunt.

"The woman that walked her beautiful Nancy to Tommy's side at that wedding was by blood kin, Aunt Betsy. By her heart, she was Nancy's Mama. Poor babe been passed around until finally Betsy and her husband, Tom Sparrow, raised Nancy as their own. Called their home 'the Sparrow's nest.' May just be that the one thing we can come to count on is to count on nothing! Time comes when a babe needs a home. With the Good Lord's tender mercies, loving hearts will make room for one more precious soul. The Sparrows done the same when Denny need a home later on. Denny was base born. He's prone to mention that to you soon after the how-do's, iffin not afore.

"Nancy was gracious and kind as the day is long, the portrait of beauty and grace as I seen it, as we all seen it. Never a harsh word to no one, never one directed at her, she was like that. Could stay with a family and blend right in. Was passed off for a time to a well-to-do family, name of Berry, I recall it. The Berry's had slaves. Fact, there were slaves cooking and serving, some fiddling too, at the very wedding of Thomas Lincoln and Nancy Hanks. Was done on the Berry's property.

"Nancy wasn't blessed with the roots I got by being under Christopher and Hannah Bush. We Bushes were plentiful, and stuck with one another like honey to a critter's paw. We were fortunate when I look round. No figuring for what become of families. Nancy was dears with a girl I know'd some - name was Sarah Mitchell. She is the woman Nancy named little Sairy after, not me, as some have said.

"Sarah Mitchell was a girl of the clearing, such as myself. Her Pa swam the Ohio trying to get his baby girl back from them Injins that were paddling off with her. She seen him drown afore she was ripped from all she known. She come back years later as part of a trade with the Injins - Abe told me it was called a treaty. What those two spoke of when they were alone, Nancy and Sarah, only the good Lord knows it. They had the same eyes, sad and still somehow at peace too. Abe got them eyes too, from Nancy no doubt.

"Nancy could ease my mind, comforted me without so much as a word, that was a gift from the Lord, for certain. I was an uppity horse, kicking and blustering for attention, times I just needed Nancy Hanks to stand by my stall to calm me down. She seen into people without a lick of judgement to her. She seen what folks need. It was Nancy that started Abe on books. He worked on the alphabet with her til he got up to simple sentences like, 'No man may put off the law of God.' Or, 'The way of God is no ill way.' It wasn't long before he mastered those and begun to take his turn during the family's daily Bible readings.

"Tom said it was a waste of time but Nancy kept urging Abe to study. 'Abe,' she'd say, 'you learn all you can, and be of some account.' And she'd tell him stories about George Washington, and said that the good Virginny blood Abe had in him was just as good as Washington's blood. Maybe she stretched things some, but it done Abe good. Nancy was never far when Abe was around. Abe and his mother are in Heaven I have no doubt, and I want to go there, go where they are. God bless Nancy."

Here the old lady stopped—turned around & cried—wiped her eyes.

Compassion overtook me and seeing that Mrs. L. needed comfort, I extended my hand to her, which she received graciously. I offered up a short prayer:

> *The Lord giveth, the Lord taketh away.*
> *His judgments are true and righteous altogether.*
> *Blessed be the name of the Lord.*

Mrs. Lincoln continued:

"Abe sent a letter to Parson David Elkins in Kaintuck, asking him to come and preach a memorial service for his Ma. I wasn't there that day of course, but I seen Parson Elkins back in Kaintuck. He's a right fine preacher. His words could be heard clearly from a quarter mile away. Happened one Sunday morning. Elkins came over to Indiana, about one year after they laid Nancy to rest. Preached a funeral sermon. Settlers all round assembled, some ride horseback a hundred wilderness miles. Folks stood about the Lincoln cabin, and from there proceeded to the tree beneath which Nancy's body was laid to rest. There stood the old minister, the lonely husband, and the two motherless children.

"That was November of 1819, so it wasn't long after that Tom lit out for Kaintuck. Abe told me later they know'd that his Pa went to get a new wife, but they didn't think he'd have any luck being as poor as he was, and with two children to raise. Abe didn't count on a danged fool such as myself!

LIVE AS I HAVE TAUGHT YOU

Back in my childhood,
the earliest days of my being able to read,
I got hold of a small book,
'Weem's Life of Washington.'
I remember all the accounts there
given of the battle fields
and struggles for the liberties of the country,
and none fixed themselves upon
my imagination so deeply
as the struggle at Trenton, New-Jersey.
The crossing of the river;
the contest with the Hessians;
the great hardships endured at that time,
all fixed themselves on my memory more
than any single revolutionary event;
I recollect thinking then, boy even though I was,
that there must have been something more
than common that those men struggled for.

More than Common

"With a bit of charcoal Abe took to writing on the puncheon floor, fence rails - he would even scrape clean the wooden fire shovel at times. I got paper in Gentryville, and Denny made ink out of blackberry briar root. Kind of ornery ink that was. Denny got so he could cut good pens out of turkey buzzard quills. It pestered Tom a heap to have Abe writing all over everything thataway, but Abe was just wrapped up in it. If he wasn't reading he was writing. Tom got mad at his marking the house up so Abe took to marking trees that Tom wanted to cut down.

"Once Abe wrote his name for me in the sand at the deer lick. 'Mama,' he says, 'that's Abraham Lincoln. Look at that, will ya? That stands for me. Don't look a blamed bit like me!'"

The old lady is amused—further apologies for her meandering monologue. She continued:

"Betsy and Dennis off on their own seem to hasten romance. Sairy married Aaron Grigsby and moved into a cabin two miles south of Tommy and me. Grigsby's were a right prominent family in the area. The wedding was joyful. Abe wrote a poem for his sister on the occasion. Colonel Chapman'll get it for ya if you want it write it down. Figuring as much with you scratching that paper with your pen as you are, no doubt wasting daylight on a bumfuzzled old lady's memories."

Abraham Lincoln recited this poem at his sister's wedding in 1826 under the title, Adam and Eve's Wedding Song (W.H.H.).

When Adam was created, he dwelt in Eden's shade,
As Moses has related, before a bride was made,
Ten thousand times ten thousand of creatures swarmed around,
Before a bride was formed, or any mate was found.

He had no consolation, but seemed as one alone,
Till, to his admiration, he found he'd lost a bone,
This woman was not taken from Adam's head, we know;
And she must not rule over him, 'tis evidently so.
This woman was not taken from Adam's feet, we see;
And she must not be abused, the meaning seems to be.
This woman, she was taken from under Adam's arm;
And she must be protected from injury and harm.
This woman, she was taken from near to Adam's heart,
By which we are directed that they should never part.
To you, most loving bridegroom, to you most loving bride,
Be sure you live a Christian and for your house provide.
Avoiding all discontent, don't sow the seed of strife,
As is the solemn duty of every man and wife.

During the interim of the above transcription, an aggrieved infant is brought to Tildy, a stop short of the arms of Granmarm Lincoln. There placed, the tender babe felt the sureness of her hold, ratcheting down from her exhortations to the deep inhale/exhale of peaceful slumber. Mrs. Lincoln continues, babe in arms:

"This here little lady come to us on account of my Matilda here. She become the bride of a Mr. Squire Hall. They give me eight grandchillern, mostly more beautiful girls. By juckies, grandbabies got old enough to bring on their babes for Granmarm. The Good Lord mussin be in no hurry for my troubles!

"After these mess makers done their magic, life ain't so free. Young love come along once. Didn't see much of my girls after they were married and gone. Abe was in his books. Poor John D. was the last one to seed off and blow away. With their hunting and fishing, John D. was right attached to Tommy. They were like blood kin, same way me and Abe were like blood kin. Tommy and Johnny were both whittling types - countryside was full of them. I reckon Abe being that near to both of them put them down some, though neither would fess to it. They'd die sooner than say so.

"I'm sorry to say John D. fell right up close to the trunk of the Daniel Johnston tree. I tried to speak to Johnny, Mr. Herndon, tried to get him thinking. There wasn't much supposing sometimes with him. He was born tired just like his Pa, and willing to walk a country mile to avoid ten feet of honest work. But I tried all I could and then done it all over again, usually managing to make matters worse when Johnny couldn't stomach his medicine.

"We saw little of Abe round bout the time he got hold of Parson Weem's story of General George. Abe got hold of that book by way of a neighbor, a Mr. Josiah Crawford."

Here I informed Mrs. Lincoln I have a deposition scheduled with the widow of the same Josiah Crawford—further east in Indiana.

"Mrs. Crawford was right saintly, Mr. Herndon. Sairy was the the maid of all work for her. Mrs. Crawford seen to Sairy as a Mama does. Abe was employed by the Crawfords at the same time. Them two was prone to follow the other it seem, bonded from Abe's first breath. I reckon still what they whispered about as young'uns pretending to be sleeping, as young'uns do. Now 'afore I get too lost, having you to remind me of my thoughts, I'll say Abe's first business in Crawford's employ was daubing the cabin, which was built of unhewn logs with the bark still on. In the loft of this house Abe slept for many weeks at a time, finished by his own hands. Spent his evenings as he did at home, with pages out of books.

"Mr. Crawford, for the love a truth, was most a time rough as a cow's tongue. Abe come to change Josiah Crawford's name to Old Blue Nose. That man was powerful peculiar in his looks. Abe wasn't for him, but would tolerate just about anything for them books. Long ago Abe tired of getting his miserable wages docked whenever he happened to lose a few minutes a steady work. Abe's pay as I can recall it was twenty five cents a day. For Crawford's books he's put up with about anything. Finally he got the gumption to ask Mr. Crawford if he could borrow a book in particular.

"So it was that Old Blue Nose let Abe borrow Parson Weem's Life of Washington. Crawford browbeat him purty good about taking care of it afore he finally done his kindness. Walking home with that book tight under his arm, Abe was happy as pig in warm mud, read this book far into the night and tucked it into a chink between the logs in the wall afore falling asleep. Pick it back up soon as the Good Lord opened his eyes again. Went on like that for some time.

"Come a driving rainstorm one night and soaked the mortar through to General George. Mr. Herndon, when Abe showed me his book it looked like he gone dipped his face in snow, my boy was white with fear. Powerful despaired at the thought of facing Old Blue Nose over it. He asked my counsel, I said there wasn't much else to do but make a clean airing of the affair, for he couldn't bring it back. Truth was, Mr. Josiah Crawford was the kind a man who'd skin a flea for its hide, and I reckoned Abe was in for tongue whacking. I said to Abe generally as these go, it done more punishment fretting silly over it than the whacking itself. Best to just git, be over and done.

"Abe said he come up to the Crawford house presenting a sorry appearance generally. He proceeded to untie the handkerchief in which the source of his distressing lay. Abe lay it down, said he couldn't hear his voice over his pounding heart! Somehow he eek out the words bout how the rain beat in and wet it through and it is spiled (Writer ascertains, "spoiled.") Abe expressed his regrets, was very sorry indeed.

"Crawford didn't spare Abe no kindness nor grace a'tall. He took the bark clear off the tree on poor Abe. But the damage was done. Having no money, Abe offered pay back in work and Crawford put him to stripping leaves off the corn for cattle fodder, for three days. Abe give him the book back, but Crawford plague Abe, suggesting it was naught more than kindling now. Flung it back at Abe and urged him to use it for fire. Abe turned and just run away. Told his yarn soon as he come a-loping home. He throwed his legs over the top a that split rail fence. When his foot seem to just touch the good earth beneath he was already firing his yarn. Abe was done with Old Blue Nose thereafter, but he owned his first book outta it!

The time come when Abe got his revenge for all the petty brutality from Old Blue Nose. Abe levelled his attacks in rhyme and chronicle and gave Old Blue Nose fame as wide as to the Wabash and the Ohio. When it left our cabin, it traveled as far as it did and come all the way back, it begun to peck at me some. I stir up hell with a long spoon over it, made it clear to Abe that I didn't like he used his gifts and done harm with them. Though I can say what scarcely one woman, especially a mother, has said a thousand times over, and it is this: Abe never gave me a cross word or look and never refused in fact, or even in appearance, to do anything I requested him. He was dutiful to me always, he loved me truly I think, so he done his best to stifle his rhymes about Old Blue Nose. Mostly it wasn't no use, even Abe couldn't unring a bell.

"Was a spectacle to see Abe when he was not eyeing his treasure a pages. I'd ask him to explain all about his book. Was the only way I was to hear his voice it seemed. I'd concoct somewheres in my fool head a question such like, 'I always heard that Washington made them redcoats run for life. Why were they called redcoats?' Abe said it was because they wore coats of that color. I expect that they looked splendid, though they likely didn't feel very splendid after they got whupped. One night as we set by the fire, I wanted to hear my boy speak his thoughts, so I fire a question at Abe about why them men would march ragged such they leave bloody footprints in snow, and I said to Abe, 'Such privations! They'd been better off not fighting a'tall I reckon.'"

"Well, that lit quite a fire under Abe. He spoke with a look like fury in his eyes, saying there was a cause far greater than comfort. My dear boy spoke of the greater part of Christendom as a mess of horrors, of bloody wars atween kings and queens. Spoke of the mass of people crushed to the earth with a bayonet right under them. Garments of their children soaked in blood. I can recite his words he said them nuff and I turn them over in my memory nuff. Would you like me to recite, Mr. Herndon?"

Rewarded for my encouragement – the old woman stands without assistance, returns the sleeping babe to Tildy – speaks:

"And here, merciful God! What scenes are rising before the eyes of horror-struck imagination? Mamas mute with grief, and looking through swelling tears on their boys, as they gird on the hated swords—shaking with strong fits, and, with their little children, filling their houses with lamentations for tearing themselves away for the dismal war, whence they are to return no more!" (Mrs. Lincoln returns to her chair)

"I known right then, Mr. Herndon. Abe was going to be a great man some day. I never let the children pester him; wasn't to have him hindered."

Mrs. Lincoln requests Chapman retrieve Abe's copy of Weem's Life of Washington. Upon inspection I asked Mrs. L. if she would permit me to transcribe a portion. My question unanswered, I discover she sleeps now. My attention is focused upon a passage underscored by the famous stepson of present company, the faded lines beneath the text are my guide. It reads:

"Hear the voice of the Divine Founder of your republic from the lips of his servant Washington. Above all things hold dear your national union.

Accustom yourselves to estimate its immense, its infinite value to your individual and national happiness. Look on it as the palladium of your tranquility at home; of your peace abroad; of your safety; of your prosperity; and even of that very liberty which you so highly prize!

To this you are bound by every tie of gratitude and love to God or man. The eyes of long oppressed humanity are now looking up to you as to her last hope;

the whole world are anxious spectators of your trial; and with your behaviour at this crisis, not only your own, but the destiny of unborn millions is involved. Your triumph will be complete: and the pressure of the present difficulties, instead of weakening will give a firmer tone to the federal government, that shall probably immortalize the blessings of liberty to our children and children's children."

The old woman awakened just as I scratched out the last few words, refreshed and, it seemed, renewed. Blinked her eyes rapidly, smiled in the direction of my voice, continued as though uninterrupted:

"Abe come out from his pages when his sister Sairy got with child. We were but a few miles apart from the Grigsbys. Belonged to the same church, and our young'uns attended the same school. When our little Sairy wanted to marry Aaron Grigsby, was right natural. Aaron's Pa was Mr. Reuben Grigsby. Aaron was his oldest of the sixteen. Sixteen chillern! Can you imagine that Mr. Herndon? His Ma and Pa made sure Aaron got good schooling. The Grigsbys regarded themselves as belonging to the 'upper ten' class, since they lived in a two-story, hewed-log house. Tommy liked to say they fancied themselves Princes of the Backwoods. They were good to Sairy is what I know'd.

"Sairy never knew her brother's fame. She was buried with her babe in her arms in the Little Pigeon Baptist Church cemetery. Aaron ran for his parent's house when Sairy begun borning - complications from the git. Eventually Sairy was loaded onto a sled and taken to the Grigsby home. A doctor and several midwives were finally called, but it was too late. Us Lincolns never know'd of it til she passed. Her child, a boy, was stillborn. I found Abe at the smokehouse soon as I got news of it, and when I told him he sat down in the doorway and buried his face in his hands. His frame shook with sobs and tears that slowly trickled from between his bony fingers as he cried.

"'They let her lay too long,' was all the words he could muster."

At this, Mrs. Lincoln voice broke and she choked with feelings. She gathered herself, continued:

"To my last day I will pine to be by Sairy's side to comfort her. I felt like somewheres, somehow, I done let Nancy down."

What reserve of strength Mrs. L. relied upon to remain composed a moment ago has evaporated. She weeps freely.

"Aaron loved Sairy, I know'd it and she know'd it. Maybe there was some blundering that night. I don't see it for blaming. Tommy and Abe forged their grief into swords. The way they reckon it, the Grigsbys thought we Lincolns shouldn't be consulted as we weren't somehow worthy. I know'd it was torture for them, such a thing would peck at a person's soul, longing for Sairy as they were. Course it was more memories of Nancy, and they were prone to fret about what might have been different. Walked round like they swallowed fire. The day Tommy died, God rest his Blessed soul, I was grateful he never learned in his living years that Sairy called for him the night she went, her and her babe. Good Lord a-Mighty, I wish'd I'd a never learned.

"Time pass on with the hurt festering when it come up the Grigsbys were putting on a double wedding. Two of their sixteen plan to marry on a single day for quite an infare it seem, 'ceptin we Lincoln's weren't invited. Tom and Abe seen it that the Grigsbys were expressing that Sairy was all gone. It burn them up plenty, and now they were ready to pick up them swords. Seem to confirm too that them Grigsbys were of a mind they's better than us Lincolns. I wasn't sure I could contain much of a thing. Was plumb sure the affair would blow clear to glory afore we were done with it. Dadgumit, I was scared for a coming murder trial! Sairy was cold in the grave so I stood Tommy and Abe both up with that, scolding them roundly and telling them I ain't planning to bury either of them right next to her.

"Abe's only weapon then was a turkey buzzard quill. Put his poison on paper, same as he done to Josiah Crawford. He wrote up something awful, unmentionable, and right fine by me, for it didn't involve a trigger. Though it was still for me to ride him some that it read like Psalm."

The good old lady had not proceeded far when she blushed beet red. Paused. "Abe took up the subject of a mix up on the wedding night of that Grigsby infare."

Mrs. Lincoln attempted to repeat some verses but could not continue for it was hardly decent – she insisted. She proposed to tell them to Tildy, who would relay them to me. Mrs. Lincoln however, was none too proper to enjoy some ribald verse, as her daughter superfluously pivots to me to repeat her Mother's titillated whispers:

"Now there was a man," begins the chronicle in question, "whose name was Reuben, and the same was very great in substance in horses and cattle and swine, and a very great household. It came to pass when the sons of Reuben grew up that they were desirous of taking to themselves wives..." it continued reverently enough. Until, hilariously I suggest, other occurances:

I will tell you a Joke about Jewel and Mary.
It is neither a Joke nor a Story.
For Reubin and Charles have married two girls,
But Billy has married a boy.
The girlies he had tried on every Side
But none could he get to agree.
All were in vain he went home again
And since that he's married to Natty.

So Billy and Natty agreed very well
And mama's well pleased at the match.
The egg it is laid but Natty's afraid.
The Shell is So Soft that it never will hatch,
But Betsy, she said, you Cursed bald head
My Suitor you never Can be.
Beside your low crotch proclaims you a botch
And that never Can answer for me.

"Miserbal as Abe was, I reckon it wasn't enough for the mending of his soul to just write it down. He dropped the poem at a point on the road where he was sure one of the Grigsbys would find it. Just as it was with Josiah Crawford, I fretted most at Abe putting his gifts to the Devil's work.

"I begun to squirm like a worm on hot ashes. There wasn't no averting what come next, so I figure any volleys that warn't hot lead were a release. Mostly I just know'd I was plumb scared. Them Grigsbys were wild with a rage, just as Abe hoped, and would be satisfied only when a Lincoln's face should be pounded into jelly and a couple of ribs cracked by some member of the injured family. Pigeon Creek code of honor demanded that somebody should be thumped in public for an outrage so grievous. Billy Grigsby wasn't foolish enough to take on Abe, so he elected to challenge John D. I was powerless nohow. The challenge came from the Grigsbys and so a fight was ordered, and a ring was marked out on the ground selected, a mile and a half from Gentryville.

"Bullies for twenty miles around attended. The friends of both parties were present in force. Abe said John started out with fine pluck and spirit but in a little while Billy got in some clever hits. Abe was all along anxiously casting about for some way to break the ring. John was fairly down and Billy on top and all the spectators cheering, swearing and pressing up to the very edge of the ring. Just then Billy Grigsby's friend William Bolen come into the ring, mostly from the general rukus of it all, but Abe seen his chance, yelling, 'Bill Bolen shows foul play!' He jumped inside the circle, grabbed Billy Grigsby by the seat of the pants and scruff of the neck and threw him into the air so hard Billy went sailing out of the ring over the heads of the spectators. The fall nearly killed him. Billy's friends picked him up and carried him off aways. Having righted John and cleared the battleground of all opponents, Abe swung a whiskey bottle.

"Seems nobody of the Grigsby faction, not one in that large assembly of bullies, cared to encounter the sweep of Abe's long and muscular arms. He was master of the lick. So much poison run through his veins that he still was not content, was told he vaunted himself in the most offensive manner, singling out the clearly beaten Billy Grigsby. Billy meekly said he did not doubt that Abe could whup him, but that if Abe would make things even between them by fighting with pistols, he would not be slow to grant him a meeting. The pistol was all that was left, Mr. Herndon. I was shy of my own shadow for some time."

Mrs. Lincoln is again upset by the circumstances, as though the crisis was present. Requires a few minutes to compose herself. Continues:

"Abe told me when General George was fourteen he was hankering for adventures and felt a strong desire to go to sea. His Ma said straight up that she could not bear to part with her son and young George's trial must have been very severe. His trunk of clothes already on board the ship, his honour in some sort pledged, his boyhood companions departing. Abe liked to say, 'His whole soul was panting for the promised pleasures of the voyage.' The Good Lord whispered to that boy, 'Honor thy mother, and grieve not the spirit of her who bore thee.' George saw the last boat going with several of his friends on it. When he saw the flash, and heard the report of the signal gun for sailing, and the ship rounding off for sea, canvas sails snapping, it was tough on George to bear it. But he done what he done for his Mama.

"Mrs. Washington begged her son to stay, such as any mother would. I had to beg my boy to go, to go far away."

I believe I am kindly enough in nature

and can be moved to pity and to pardon

the perpetrator of almost the worst

crime that the mind of man can conceive

or the arm of man can execute;

but any man, who,

for paltry gain can rob Africa of her children

to sell into interminable bondage,

I never will pardon,

and he may stay and rot in jail

before he will ever get relief from me.

Rob Africa of Her Children

"James Gentry lived afore the railroads, markets were a ways off. Mr. Gentry earned himself a heap, owned five thousand acres of land. Was the first to the area and called it after himself. So Gentryville, Indiana come about. James was southern by his nature, born in North Carolina, married in Kaintuck, settled in Indiana. A regular North Star! He done right by his family with his smarts and his energy. Cared for his neighbors generally, good hearted that way. Come to find out we could grow cotton, so Gentry got himself a cotton gin, of all things. Think we were deep South! He shared it, not looking to loot no one over it. He done fine sending flat boats south with corn and hogs mostly, down the Ohio and Mississipp to New Orleans. Thirteen hunnerd miles if you were counting, that's what Abe said. So I done my snooping and sure enough, James was planning to send his boy Allen captaining cargo down river, and soon. That boy as I know'd him then had a good heart and keen mind, just like his Pa. Way I figure it, that's where Abe needed to be. So I wait till I seen James, so as not to plague the idea.

"When I seen him at a raising, like most people were at the time, James speak of this business with the Grigsbys. I was torn up about it generally. Seem the whole henhouse was a-cluck over it. I said to him, 'As I seen it, Abe needs to git some distance from this trouble with the Grigsbys.'

"James think on it a minute and come up on it with his eyes bright, he says, 'Maybe Abe outta get on that flatboat with Allen.'

"Why, James, that's a right fine idea, if he'll go for it."

"James says, 'A course he will,' and he goes on to speak of the adventures and sights Abe'd get to see going down river.

"So I thunk out loud on it, spoke as if it was just like them stories Abe liked to read about in his books all the time. James shine on this thought, says he figures he'll mention it. And so it was. Allen and Abe were gonna wait till they got the seed in and the crop start breaking ground, and then they were gonna git.

"Mr. Herndon, you must excuse me but I must say, Lady that I am, that it could not escape me—the irony. Right quick, Allen married Katey Roby and the trip done got put off till the borning of her babe the following December. Seems how we make plans and the Good Lord gets Himself tickled purple over it.

"Just as well, Abe settled rightfully with the Grigsbys. In time he took kindly to my nudging him and he know'd his poison ain't done nothing to bring Sairy back, or help himself. Grigsbys owned the only good grindstone several miles round so folks brung their tools to sharpen. Reuben's bride, name of Betsy, easy for me to recall these many years later, she turned the grindstone. Abe wait his turn afore he said, when it come, 'Let me do it for you, Betsy.'

"She seen the gesture for what it was and was right pleased to get a rest from such drudgery. She step back and leave Abe to handle the job. Only when he sharpened his axe did Abe allow Betsy Grigsby to return. Just then Natty Grigsby said, 'It's all over now.' Natty been torn up specially over the whole affair, as him and Abe were together most often. From then the hard feelings betwixt the Grigsbys and Abe seem to melt away like snow in spring.

"Allen and Katey's baby come along—a boy—and they name him James after his grandpappy. Was too soon for me when the day finally come for Allen and Abe to shove off. I dreaded that sunrise like none other, and I know'd that dread ever since. I never seen Abe the same since the day I seen him off then. Felt as I swallowed a goose, feathers and all.

"That flatboat shove off loaded corner to corner with sacks and barrels, and critters, mostly caged and corralled. The craft was built like Abe, long and narrow. It was somewheres round eighty foot long and near twenty across. Allen was at the front, with an oar for steering, and Abe was in the back with a long oar meant for push. James paid Abe eight dollars a month. Think Abe would pay James to go if he asked it that way. My boy was starving for the outside world.

"Took them five days on the Ohio, and then most of the next month on the Mississipp. Abe said the trick was to stay on top of the deepest part of the river he could find, keep the river bottom from slowing them down. Ohio's got plenty of riffles (Writer ascertains—translate as "ripples") to contend with. Abe seen mostly land as the Good Lord made it. Said forest hung down over cliffs and he reckon he could see some of them hairy elephants again. He was fooling on me some I spect, but it must a been a real spectacle to see the herds and flocks roaming and flying as they done since Creation. Abe said folks sprung up here and there. Seen buildings the size of ten of the courthouse in Liztown, back in Kaintuck. Was for storing cargo along the river, tobaccy and such. Abe seen free Negros living up with the Shawnee, can you imagine Mr. Herndon?

Some journeys end right where the Ohio meets the Mississipp. Figure it mussin a been a wild ride with them two bullies running into the other, crafts tossed and turned, send their goods to fend for themselves. Men left fishing out what they can and walking home, feeling their pride hurt somewhat. Other men were living off the river banks, gathering up the driftwood from the busted up flatboats, turn round and sell it to the steamboats for firewood. Abe said they were river rats of a sort. He seen things along the banks he was sure not to tell his Mama. Was temperate in all things. Still steal some of the boy right out of him once put afore his eyes. He wasn't all boy no more, and never could be again.

"Abe said the Mississipp was wider and muddier than the Ohio, men call it Big Muddy cause of it. Big Muddy seem to be in no hurry, Abe said, curving throughout the country like it did. Wished he could straighten it, said it would half his trip. Further south he got, less it was like home. Abe saw houses that looked like courthouses, with white columns. Moss hung from the trees. Rows and rows of slave shacks scattered round a big house. Passed Vicksburg, Abe did, where General Grant was to hold seige on his brothers and sisters some years later on. I reckon Abe thought back on his trips on the Mississipp when he was warring over it in the years later.

After a prolonged silence, Mrs. Lincoln continued:

"It's a wonder what those boys spoke of as they were going down river, day after day. Comment on what they seen, for certain. It's a wonder what those boys spoke on the topic of Ms. Katey, Mama to Allen's baby. So many unasked questions Mr. Herndon. Too, too, many.

"Katey could see past Abe's all round protruding features. Not all of them could. Was a time Abe was laying with Katey on the banks of the Ohio, he was to fondly recall how they would look up at the stars. Once she said the moon was on its way down. Abe says, 'That ain't so' and he jump off to speak of how the earth was spinning. He was so particular and sure about what he know'd. Seemed to me from Abe's yarn that Ms. Katey appreciated Abe as he should be. He was right what he said of the earth spinning, a course. Must a come to Katey years later that she find Abe was right all along. Seemed to me Abe put a shine on Katey, seeing she enjoyed his speeching as she did. She chose Allen."

Mrs. L. has a few questions of her own, with my permissions inquired how my friendly acquaintances and family members refer to Writer. I inform her that Mr. L. liked to refer to me as 'Billy.' She enjoys this very much, requests permission to call me the same. I grant it with pleasure, surrendering my last vestiges of objectivity.

"Billy," she repeats to her delight, and inquires of my children. I tell her of my oldest, and that she has not left our home for a prolonged period, though she would like to at the earliest opportunity, and with the greatest passion. This delights Mrs. L. I return her attention to the subject of her son. She pauses, acclimating with great effort.

"It's a might chilly in here, don't you think?" she said to Colonel Chapman. Her assessment was a source of astonishment to Writer.

"How about a cup of tea, nice and hot, Granmarm?" Chapman asked, rising to put another log on the modest fire. She nodded eagerly and he turned to me. "Mr. Herndon?"

"Yes, indeed," I replied. "Thank you."

Tildy appears at Sarah's side, ministering to her comfort. Warming Sarah's hands with her own, Tildy hugs the old woman without pause. I was unexpectedly and suddenly longing for the company of his own mother. The Peace, Strength and Glory of God be with you always my good Mother! After multiple sips of honey tea, Mrs. L. is refreshed.

"My Tildy spiles me with her Blessed heart." After a moment with Tildy I remind Mrs. Lincoln of our topic, Abe departing to New Orleans. She went on:

"The flatboat was tied up for the night as they were nearing New Orleans. The boys were awakened by a ruckus along the shoreline. Abe shouted, 'Who's there?' He often described the brief quiet when it wasn't clear what was to occur. Abe said his belly tighten any time just by retrieving the incident from his memories, all them years later. Just then a gang of escaped slaves storm onto Abe and Allen's craft carrying clubs. Allen had his Pa's wits, and he shouted out "Bring the guns, Abe! Shoot them!" But they had no guns, Allen just made them believe in it. By now Abe's got himself a handspike and knocked over the first, second, third, and fourth, in turn, when the remaining few took to the woods. The boys chased them off afore they cut their ties and float on. Abe had a scar from it over his eye, had it still when he come see me that final time.

"As they got closer to New Orleans they would pull ashore lingering and get pricing, plantation after plantation, mostly slave cabins and fields of sugar cane. Soon enough they arrived. Abe said they seen it at night, like a giant kettle fire a ways off. The city was lit up like they had torches burning on every corner, 'ceptin instead of a torch it was a lantern lighting up by fish blubber, fish called a whale, and the whale was at times as big as a whole ship. Quite a world beyond my old candlesticks and tallow dips, Billy! Abe brung it to me, just fine for him to see it and tell me all about it than for a clearing lady such as me to git out for myself.

"Abe said they stopped when the flatboats and steamers were lining up both sides of the river, sometimes four deep, boats tied up together. Some were sold out, while the one next was loaded up. Then come a wall between the river and the city with a broad flat area on top. Men unload cargo from the flatboats, fill up the pushcarts, three or four barrels at a time, offin for the city or the steamboats. Horse and wagon pass freely on top of the wall, call it a levee. Abe said the air hardly moved, filled with the smoke from the cooking fires. Smell of food was all around like he'd never smell it and felt it afore. Eyes burn while his stomach rumbles.

"The steamboats were filling the time rumbling and hissing like it where ten fields of snakes. Can you imagine that Billy? All the while alongside the squealing and squawking livestock on the flatboats. Whole world coming together there, climbing up and down the steps of that levee. Allen was of course in a mood to get back to his newborn son and wife, so they sold what was left in New Orleans and come back home by steamboat. Abe got it in his head for a time afterwards that he might captain such a ship. Made quite an impression on my boy.

"A Merciful Lord finally deliverd Abe to my door again. He stooped under the doorway and unfurled himself to me as I dreamt it every day he was away. I brung him to me and swore then that I wasn't gonna release him again, and kept my hold on him. He was mightily amused by this, Billy, and it reached into my heart about as deep as it go, to feel him grinning such whilst I had him snug. Like squeezing a tree branch hugging that boy was.

"Seemed like right soon after Abe returned that the milk sick come back to Pigeon Creek, and the news from Illinois was a land a black soil. Tommy wasn't one for milk sick, he know'd his heart couldn't take no more after Nancy. He was a fool too for the promise of a new land where the living was somehow appearing to be less plagued than this one. We were off just when the frost is coming out of the ground, which made it plenty muddy for driving four yoke of oxen. We find our way through daily trials. Abe help us build this here cabin and then he was off again for New Orleans.

"Abe was independent age that second trip. Was his life now. This time my John D. was going with Abe. Spite his gumption, he was a babe once in my arms. Saying goodbye to my boys was trial worthy of the wicked. Daily I carry on feeling as through there were embers in my gullet. John Hanks, who was Nancy's cousin from Kaintuck, fancy the idea and declared he would go along too. Pleased me so that Nancy and I should both have our represents with Abe on that trip, like we were both there in flesh and blood. Nancy like it too, I spect. Nancy is in Heaven I have no doubt, and I want to go there, go where she is, God bless Nancy.

"John Hanks, as I recall it, was the one to find a man who was going to supply the cargo and boat. Departing from Springfield, Illinois. First I heard of the place. Man's name sound just like one with big plans —name of Denton Offutt. Ain't that a name for a man who's out to make all kind a things happen? 'Ceptin when they track him down at a tavern, he's full a whiskey, speeching on to the assembled, also full a whiskey. Abe said he spoke flourishgly of Andrew Jackson. Abe's new partner had plenty of speeches, and no boat neither. Welcome to the world, Abe Lincoln!

"Mr. Offut, he sent the boys off toward government timber and said if they want a boat, he reckons they should make it. Sure nuff they done it. Went to hauling goods on the river, hogs and corn again mostly. Five of them set off, including Mr. Denton Offut. He was eager to spend his earnings in New Orleans. Lordy, Lordy, what sin he'd find without much bother, not that he bother. John Hanks jumped off at Saint Louis and come home. Just like Nancy, he wasn't to see the journey to its end.

"With both my boys gone, I was sick every day, could not manage much solid. A Mama's heart faces many perils. They stay a full month in New Orleans. Mr. Denton Offut was in no hurry to return home with the earnings like Allen Gentry was that first trip. Day finally come after that when I see them coming over yonder. Next they both go off to war together, like they were trying to kill me, it felt so. But I am a bit ahead of myself to fire that yarn just yet. This'n here is about Abe in the slaving center for a whole month. Abe took note with such wonder at how them civilized people of New Orleans could make a business of selling people just like them. He figured over it till it take him a long, long ways down his thoughts. Abe said often of the scars on his heart he got in New Orleans. Painful to speak of, Billy."

I replied to Mrs. L. that these experiences could be relevant to history. I desired to spare her the heartache, but I was compelled to share my opinion that Abe's thoughts about slavery, those wounds in his heart, could be important to the generations to come, and she was most likely the only one alive he had left those memories with. She gathered her strength, hands clenched with fistfuls of shawl, she continued:

"Abe walked the streets plenty. Slaves, free blacks, and whites mingled in the port of the Mississipp. Sights and sounds of the river delta unimaginable for an old lady from the clearing. He said New Orleans was what I known, maybe a little bigger is all. We have our log cabin church, and folks gather from all around. New Orleans has a Cathedral with a tower, maybe twice the top of the Liztown courthouse. At the top of this Cathedral was a clock big enough for all to see. Abe said a bell rung all through the day. Was where the folks gathered around. Just more of them and looking every shade a color possible. That was the best I could reckon he was saying about mulattos and ochanondos, and all kind words troubling to a small mind such as my own.

"All them roads meet in a central square at the center of town. Abe said he could cross a street and back and not come across a single word he could understand as folks were speaking their native country. Other than that, Abe said it just like Gentryville, making up the center of things for sundries and seeing other folk.

"I ask Abe once about the dress of the proud body ladies, hopeless sinners as they are. He said the ladies wear white gloves and dress in their finest cloth, like table linens, 'cept thinner, and shade or two brighter. Women were prone to wear fancy jewelry and colorful hats, some with a basket over their arms, others fancy a Negro servant to carry their basket.

"He loved to tell his Mama about the things he seen, describing harvested crops I couldn't rightly imagine. Seen something from south of America, countries Abe try and imagine. He wanted to go to Europe after he was President, wanted to take his beautiful Mary and their Blessed boys. Did you know that, Billy? Abe come across a crop that looked like green apple, but shaped like sorta like a bean. Cut open it was orange as a sunset and smelled just like a flower, and even taste like candy. Can you imagine it, Billy, such a crop? S'pose I'm down along wilderness path with my words again, for sake a sparing us the troubles. There was much shame. Abe breathe it in.

"Slave pens were scattered throughout the business district. Newspapers were filled with advertisements for sales, and auctions were taking place all around the city. Abe said they brung them poor souls out chained six together. Iron was around the left wrist of each, and this fastened to the main chain by a shorter one. Abe compare it to fish upon a trot line, the Negros were strung together so precisely like. He speak on about how they were being separated forever from anything a poor soul could cherish - mamas and wives, children, friends, and everything they ever known or were. Left without so much as a pinch a dignity, stripped naked and required to dance to show their strength and wares. He seen children taken from their Mama but he hardly spoke none on it. Trying to forget it is best of my figuring. "

Mrs. L. greatly distressed. Weeps freely. Writer joins.

"Abe seen folks in pens. Animal pens is what they were. Can you imagine it, Billy? My boy marveled when he seen them, said them Negro folk were the most cheerful and apparently happy souls. One played the fiddle almost continually while the others danced, sung, cracked jokes and played various games with cards. Ain't seen too many animals playing games with cards. Was the gravest insult to us all. Abe know'd it that way, showed me and a few others too.

"John D. told me once about an auction they seen when a beautiful girl was exhibited like a race horse, her points dwelt on one by one, in order, as the auctioneer said that bidders might satisfy themselves. Johnny said Abe's heart bled open just then, said nothing much, was off somewheres else like. Turning to the others my Abe offered a solemn oath, 'Boys, if ever I get a chance to hit that slavery, I'll hit it hard.' He bide his time, but he done it.

"He told me he seen an older Negro man and he come right out, innocent and maybe a little green about it too, and he ask the man if he was happy in slavery. The old feller unbent his back as much as possible and raising a face without a crease of hope in it and said, Abe said it just as he done, 'No—no Marse. I nevah is happy no mo. Whippin's is things that black folks nevah can stop rememberin' about—they hurt so.'

"Abe had his hardest trial around two boys same age as him. Before his eyes they were sold off by a trader to a local man. Them boys become fast friends after they were dragged away in chains together. Soon they hatch a plan and run off. Abe was quick to say he'd a done the same thing. It vexed him so that they were just like him and they were bound in slavery. Tortured him truly. A man caught one of them boys—name of Elisha, who broke free a his captor an nearly stab him to his death.

"There was no sign of the other boy, his name is long gone from my head. But they were on the trail now of Elisha, till they caught that poor, terrorized little boy. His Mama—oh, I ache over it now as I done then. If she know'd what become of her boy, she never have another moment of joy again, not a moment's peace til Judgement Day.

"Elisha got himself caught again, and they build a gallows outside his Parish Prison window. Hung him four days later. I was wishing I could say then that the other boy made it to freedom, but it ain't so. Know why, Billy? Cause he show up to see his friend hang to his death. When the trap door rip open on Elisha, stealing his last breathe, the other boy was watching along with the crowd assembled. Just then he died right along with his friend. Abe said the newspaper read the boy died of something they called 'violent spasms,' but Abe know'd, and I know'd, and you know too, Billy—that boy died of a broke heart. Abe was forged right then into a sword to be wielded by the Almighty. He was given a mission, and I curse myself, selfish as the Devil, that I just wanted him to be my son, living still, here now having tea with his friend Billy and his Mama."

Here the old lady stopped—turned around & cried.

"Abe's mind was a marvelous instrument. He figured this one would do this and that that one would do that. He knew folks. Might be he set it up just right for folks in the North to accept war as they done. They rallied for war after Abe's having the Rebs fire on us at Fort Sumter. We were fighting for Union, not for freeing Negros. Even if that's what Abe had in mind all along. Abe didn't free the slaves. They freed themselves with their fleeing feet and warring bravery. Abe just give name to it—Emancipation. He need them slaves to win the war, and we done it. Yes, Billy, his mind was a marvelous instrument to steer them narrows. In the end it was all about winning, to protect what George Washington teach him in that there Parson Weem's book from so long ago, once belong to Old Blue Nose himself, Josiah Crawford. Tee-hee-hee.

"Just like that, we didn't fight for kings and queens no more, we fight for what we believed, one way or the other. My family was from Kaintuck. They all fought for the Rebs, many died for them. Most awful horror, truly was. Our boys were killing each other. We may a had our diff'rences then, but us Mamas all got the same aching heart now. I know'd it was somehow all got to be, Abe sayin' it so.

~∾~

Abe found a way
out of every tight place
while the rest of us
were standing round
scratching our fool heads.
I reckon
Abe an Aunt Sairy
run that moving
an good thing they did
or we'd a been run into a swamp
an sucked under.

~∾~

Good Thing They Did

"It was John Hanks who got restless fust. Lit out for Illinois. Wrote for us all to come, and he'd git land for us. Tom was always itching for the land of Canaan nohow, and the land of Pigeon Creek wasn't all paid for. Then milk sick come back and it was time for goodbyes.

"Tommy and me went back to Kaintuck a last time to sell my tiny property. Sold it for one hundred and twenty-three dollars. Paid but twenty-five for it as a scared widow. Seen my kin a last time. We spent our one final evening firing yarns bout things Ma and Pa done. Talked all over their chillern with joyful introductions. The time was precious and we know'd it. Seen my Ma and Pa's graves together for the first and last time. Made my best goodbye. Wished they'd a met Abe.

"Back in Indianny Tommy handed the mortgage back over to James Gentry. Sold most of the livestock to David Turnham, I recall. Piled everything into ox wagons and we went. Lincolns and Hankses and Johnstons, all hanging together. I reckon we were like one of the tribes of Israel that you kain't break up, nohow. There were five famlies of us then.

"Was a final church service with most of the folks round. Visit to gravesites was more wrought to the core. Nancy and Sairy, and that seed of a boy all laid into ground soaked with tears. It pains me to speak of it, Billy.

"Something I want to git for you, Billy," she said, rising and making her way slowly to the bureau near the fire. Opening the top drawer, she reached in and took out a folded sheet of paper. "This here's a poem Abe wrote for me, of his return to Indiana, years later. Would you read it for me?" It was my divine pleasure to do so. I transcribe:

> My childhood home I see again,
> And gladden with this view;
> And still as mem'ries crowd my brain,

There's sadness in it too—
O memory! Thou mid-way world
'Twixt Earth and Paradise;
Where things decayed, and loved ones lost
In dreamy shadows rise—
And freed from all that's gross or vile,
Seem hallowed, pure, and bright,
Like Scenes in some enchanted isle,
All bathed in liquid light—
Now twenty years had passed away
Since here I bid farewell
To woods and fields, and scenes of play
And schoolmates loved so well—
The very spot where grew the bread
That formed my bones, I see.
How strange, old field, on thee to tread,
And feel I'm part of thee!

Mrs. L. appears ready the moment my eyes look up from the transcription above. Alert, she continues:

"It took us two weeks to git to Illinois, rafting over the Wabash, cutting our way through the woods, fording rivers, prying wagons and steers out of sloughs with fence rails. Abe made sure to joke every time he cracked a whip, and between us we found a way out of every tight place while the rest of them were standing round scratching their fool heads. I reckon Abe and me run that moving. Good thing we did, too, or it would a been run into a swamp and sucked under.

"Were three covered wagons. Women sat in a covered cart, stare at the backsides of a yoke of oxen. Was me a course, and my girls Betsy and Tildy. Their husbands were along by horseback, Denny and Squire. Chillern push as they can, or just walk along iffin able to keep the weight off the wagon. Abe strode along in the mud, driving the oxen as best he could. He was fond of wearing a felt hat round about then. It was black when he first got it, but was sunburned until it was a combine of colors. He was tall and tightly wound. Round then Abe wore a suit of blue homespun waistcoat and britches. Had a roundabout jacket. Wore boots then, he did. Too cold to do otherwise.

"The oxen were a pulling our wares through the mud and snow. We pressed on, anxious to settle on a parcel and git a crop in. Denny was speeching, seemed continuous at times. He was crowing about the sights he seen when he went out afore us to spy the land.

"Mornings were best, mud thickens as the day warms up. Times the men had to unharness all eight beasts, six ox and both horses, to have them pull one wagon at a time through the orneriest places. Men were on all corners a pushing and a heaving. Times we'd unload some of our goods right there in the wilderness, all size of people were carrying armfuls across the roughs, and then load it back up again somewheres further along, after we'd passed through it. Was a struggle at times cutting West.

"Most of the trip I spent stealing baby Johnny from Tildy. He was just a newborn still, worked his lungs plenty along the rocks and stumps bumping his ride. Fussy lil varmint! Granmarm done her best to grin up through worst of it. Johnny and I were bonded for life after that, still see him a plenty, bouncing in my door to see his Granmarm. Tildy and Squire were already up to quite a brood, four of them by then. Tildy was a right natural Mama, having John D. to keep an eye on all them years.

"Dennis fetched us some game as we went along, plentiful as the sixth day after the Good Lord finished Creation. A time come when we noticed the family dog - Abe call her 'Honey,' mostly because he seem to call all his dogs Honey - wasn't with us. Tommy, Denny, John D., and Squire, the lot of them said we must keep on going. Abe wasn't having it a'tall, and he fix us for camp and turned back, paying no mind to the menfolk's fussing no more than the little papoose on my lap. He found old Honey running up and down the river bank, too scared to cross the current, which was plenty swift. Abe crossed back over the stream and swoop up Honey and walk her back, doing his best to restrain the terrified critter and ford the stream at the same time, in the shadows of dusk by then. But he done it of course. He simply couldn't endure the idea of leaving that poor dog behind. That was the heart that beat inside my boy, Nancy's boy too. I wasn't pestered by the wait on him back then.

"Seen my Sister Hannah on the way through Illinois. She was Hannah Bush Radley by then. It was quite a time, shame it was just one night. Ain't seen her since I run off the day I married Tommy, was maybe ten years since. She had her family and I had plenty a news from Kaintuck, seeing as I had just been there.

Her kin may a had the Radley name but to look at them they were pure Bushes, even by name, John and Isaac. My brother Isaac must a been purt nigh honored with the news his sister named her boy Isaac. He spoke nothing of it to no one though, for certain.

The Radley/Bush boys were kind enough to accompany us to our land. Imagine it, Billy, them boys being there was like an escort from none other than my brothers and very own Pa. Was a Blessing from the All-Loving, Merciful and Kind. Was another three days afore we reached flat lands that were owned by no one but the blue skies and the feasting thick grass.

"Afore too long we were served up fever and winter as I had never known. Was fighting to live in this land of milk and honey. Tommy had us all going back to Indiana till my sister Hannah visit and talk some Bush sense into him. Hannah Bush Radley, none other than my Mama's namesake, gonna pass on some of her wisdom. She tell Tommy what he need to hear - the children of Israel trying to find the Promised Land, but no Red Sea divided for us yet. Times come when all sorts of difficulties beset us. We keep on the course we set.

"It was a purty country up on the Sangamon River, and we were all took up with the idea that they could run steamboats up to our cornfields and load. We moved to Coles County, and we've been here ever since. Abe helped put up a cabin for Tom and me, cleared fifteen acres for corn, and split walnut rails to fence it in. Abe was then somewheres round twenty-one. Was free to go then, had reached his age of independences, and Tommy give him some money to get what we used to call a 'freedom suit.' Abe stayed through that next spring and most of the summer to build and clear and get us set.

"When the seed was in the field, last thing Abe done was to plant me a garden of flowers. He know'd more than just vegetables. He always seen a world beyond and now it was his time. I certainly couldn't follow him so there was nothing for this lonely old woman to do 'ceptin to say goodbye. I done all I could right then not to let him go, but a course I know'd what must be.

"Abe said goodbye to his Pa, promising to send money as soon as he could. They shook hands then. Tom was hoarse and not speaking, if for only once in his life. Abe turned to me and I felt I should nearly die right then. He put his long arms around me and must a kept me from falling. Wasn't but a few blinks it was me holding that wilderness boy from feeding the forest floor. Oh Lord a-Mighty! It went too fast! He whispered to me that he's gonna see me as often as he can, and would not let a day pass that he don't think of me generally. I knew it was so, Billy, but it was sweet as honey for my ears to hear the words said. I watched him walk off, and turn and wave once more afore he clear the horizon. I look off every day still hoping to see my boy appear small in the distance. When Abe went to live away from us, we all just thought the whole world was gone. Felt so.

"Travellers were how I got the news of Abe. They were well used to bringing things about family and that, and some come across word of Abe along the way. When Tommy come back from town looking all like a cat that swallowed a bird, I know'd then that somewheres along the way he seen someone who come up on Abe. My heart wished for news of a girl who could love him as Abe should be loved, but it seemed the news was mostly about what Abe done. The Good Lord begun his sculpting on Abe with them Clary's Grove Boys. Jack Armstrong was lead wolf in a mighty awful pack. There was a lawlessness on the clearing at times. Keeping laws on the clearing was Bush family business back in Kaintuck. My Pa was a captain of the Patrollers, my brothers were Patrollers. William, Samuel, Isaac, Elijah, Junior, and John. Tommy was too, for a while, till he just couldn't bring himself to catch them slaves so close to freedom no more."

After some pause Mrs. Lincoln requests that I, "Keep an eye on Granmarm Lincoln" when she wanders off in the wilderness with her story. I promise to keep her somewhere in the direction of the core of her story, but again allowed for the enjoyment and potential value of her side reminiscences. Mrs. L. remains distressed that she appears an "old fool." Now it is my turn to console, which comforts her greatly. I remind her she speaks of the Clary's Grove Boys. She continued:

"Without a certain law yet, the clearing could become a place for thugs to have their way. There were other gangs in the area, Sand Ridge Boys, Island Grove Boys. Pure deviltry for deviltry's sake. Would put a stone under a feller's saddle just to see him get bucked when he jump on. Was for that kind of foolishness and then some. Once built a fire round a man's wooden leg, another time rolled a portly feller down a hill in a whiskey cask. Guess they were mad it was empty. But the meanest of the bunch was the Clary's Grove Boys, and the meanest of the meanest was Jack Armstrong.

"Abe was working at a store with none other than a Mr. Denton Offut, that same Mr. Offut from the second trip to New Orleans. Offut seen in Abe a goose to lay him golden eggs. Got an eye for talent, credit him so. Mostly it seemed because Mr. Offut was what my Pa would call 'the talking type' that the trouble begun, saying Abe was strongest this and the toughest that. News reach the Clary's Grove Boys as though Abe done the bragging on himself. Tommy got a glint in the eye as he hear them boys come to find out for themselves about this gangly braggart. He tussle with Abe plenty, had a pride he dare not speak for his own reasons, but he know'd how the yarn end afore it even begun.

"Jack Armstrong seen himself at the top of the heap, was looking chin high for the chance to beat on a challenger. Was a square-built feller, word was he was strong as an ox. Abe didn't want no trouble but after Offut run his mouth nothing was going to satisfy the question other than a fight. Offut hold the fight on ground near his grocery, good for sales to see my boy's life threatened, I s'pose. All a New Salem turn out, betting jack-knives and tobacco plugs over it, all of them in for Jack Armstrong. They wrestle to a draw mostly, with no one thrown. This Armstrong feller must have been all they said iffin he could fight Abe to a draw! Draw wasn't what Jack had in mind so he resorted to some foul play, grab Abe with a choke hold not permitted for wrassling. That stirred up Abe and he just as quick seized the bully by the throat and shook him like a little boy. The other members of the gang were ready to jump in and beat Abe senseless. Abe backed himself up against Offut's store, never feared none, just said in fairness he should fight em all one at a time. Something about Abe stirred a voice in none other than Jack Armstong, for he put a stop to it then. Right kindly, none other that Jack Armstrong, put his arm around Abe and took him in. Abe could find a way into the tiniest heart. Them two were bonded for life.

"Next come Chief Black Hawk, brung up the Sauk and the Fox tribes up North in Illinois. Believing as Indians do, that land can't be sold, Black Hawk simply come back and said, 'We come to plant corn.'

"That was all them settlers needed to run off to their forts, and sure enough went to war over it. Abe and John D. were off. The time they were gone put some strain on my systems, not for eating generally, though Tommy plagued me so. Think it was Tildy who handed my baby Nancy round then to save me. I tell that babe all about a girl name of Nancy Hanks. We were laughing together all over again, till I undone her crying by tending to her ever changing needs. Fussy lil varmint! Was only so long afore my thoughts turn back to them boys so far away. What if they were crying for their Mama, and me too far away to hear it? Seem like five lifetimes but it wasn't even a full season afore they showed up at my door again, tired and hungry. Nearly starved was fine - they were upright, and all they needed was some good tending-to. Wished it could be like that every day.

"After they eat their fill of Johhny cake and bacon fast as I could cook it, they begun to fire them yarns. There was no overlooking Abe Lincoln. That become clear as spring water when them boys elected him Captain of their warring unit. Abe spoke on the honor many a time. He seen for the first time that people were purty drawn to him. He pine on and on funning his many bloody struggles in battle - with mosquitoes. They didn't see much fighting, nor food neither. A poor old Injin took refuge in the camp and the men wanted to hang him. Abe stood up mad as a cornered bull and said them boys were gonna have to kill him first. My boy had no stomach for it. The Good Lord find tough rock on his chisel!

"Number of days between visits was always too long for my heart. When Abe'd come back to see us we'd hug and kiss him and try to get him to promise that he'd never go again no more. But we know'd it was no use. I think some of us know'd Abe was meant for somewhere's special.

"I made sure to set aside some meat in case Abe show up. I knew he was gonna need feeding. Someone would hear something from someone about Abe and pass it along to us. Sometimes reports would disagree and we'd spend our days puzzling over it, Tommy and me. Then come the news that Abe was gonna stand for election to be a state lawmaker of Illinois. Tommy seemed a little relieved almost when word come Abe was defeated, crowing on about how he reached too far. Made no matter to me, Abe said once that politics is short and sweet, like an old woman's dance. I didn't concern myself nohow. I was still waiting on news of a young woman. Abe seemed bent on doing and the world seem bent on him doing it.

"Just as it was when I was a daughter of Christopher and Hanna Bush back in Liztown, Abe found his way to the clearing. Spied a village alongside the Sangamon River while he was on his New Orleans visit. Place called New Salem. All Abe's yarns bout being a wheelwright, cooper, tinner, weaver and blacksmith, they remind remind me of them days in Liztown. Turns out the blacksmith had a lot of books, so Abe spent most a his time there, making the most of the idle hours when farmers were busy with their crops. Found some books in a barrel, would you believe. 'Colonel, would you fetch them books for Granmarm Lincoln? I figure Billy may find them interesting.' (Writer: Book is A complete set of Blackstone's Commentaries.) Abe purchase a log-built store. Was partners with a Mr. Berry, as I recall. Sell anything from coffee to kerosene. Tildy seem prone to whisper they sold whiskey too. No mind, the store winked out and my boy owed more money than my poor mind could figure. Abe try to make joke of it, calling it the National Debt, but there wasn't a speck of humor in it for his Mama."

Mrs. L. excuses herself, upset as though the debt crisis was present. Colonel Chapman and Tildy raise her from beneath her shoulders. She spoke of her "blood reaching her toes, steadied herself, stabilized by Col. Chapman's forearm. Tildy hovers along her mother's left side while Col. Chapman guides Mrs. Lincoln to her bedside. She lays prone after Tildy wedged coverlets beneath her mother's lower left back and neck. Propped up on pillows to 35 degrees to support her body, now fully outpaced by her mind, Mrs. Lincoln rests. Writer too breaks while Tildy removed her mother's white linen bonnet, freeing the flowing gray hair tossed upside down, curls flowing freely atop her gown collar turned down. Throughout my introductions along this journey, Mrs. Lincoln was commonly described by acquaintances as 'straight as an Indian.' This long and wiry frame produced much over many years. A great beauty still. Laying prone, hair freed, was true and genuine comfort and material aid to Mrs. L. She continued:

"John D. married a woman by name of Mary Barker round the harvest of 1834, as I recall it. Somewheres round then I reckon. Mary was as a woman should be on her wedding day. I saw much in her, making the same mistake I made with the groom's dearly deceased Pa. My boy was a charmer, and handsome as his Pa. Poor little Mary Barker had stars in her head where her eyes should be. Betsy and Tildy were there with Denny and Squire, and their restless gang a grandchildren. My Sister Hannah was there with her family of Bush children. Tommy was right jolly, he thunk the world of my Johnny. They were like blood kin same way me and Abe were. Abe wasn't there for Johnny's day, but I know'd he would have been at Johnny's side if word had reached him in time. Them two had many an hour together in fields and wilderness, in the loft with their whispering, been to New Orleans and back together. If Abe had known, he'd a been there.

"News come round that Abe was a postmaster in New Salem. Meant he could read all the newspapers in his shirt sleeves with his feet up on the counter. Traveler come by and told Tildy that Abe would stick letters in his hat to deliver them. Would read the letter for folks when necessary, write a reply for them sometimes. See what Nancy Hanks done all them years ago by teaching her boy? Round then Abe also got to surveying land, anything to earn money without a heavy instrument of force. Abe was fond to say, 'My father taught me to work, but he did not teach me to like it.'

"Day come when I thought I'd surely die as Abe Lincoln stood afore my door wearing a new suit made of butternut jeans, woolen socks, and buckskin jacket. Seem Abe was meeting new folks all the time and sure enough, next time around my boy was elected state lawmaker. I was right proud and figured now why there was no talk of a girl, Abe ain't met her yet was all. He was loping along for bigger places.

"Abe told me he become a lawyer. He said it only after we were grinning a plenty about a yarn he spun about a minister and lawyer. Abe done it better, but it went somewheres like this a way:

'A minister and a lawyer were riding along the countryside. Says the minister to the lawyer, 'Sir, do you ever make mistakes in pleading?'

'I do', says the lawyer.

'And what do you do with mistakes?' asks the minister.

'Why sir,' says the lawyer. 'If large mistakes come, I mend them. If small ones, I let them go.' The lawyer then returned the inquiry for the minister. 'And pray sir, do you ever make mistakes in your preaching?'

'Yes sir I have,' replies the preacher. Of course, the lawyer has his real question all lined up now. 'And what,' he asks, 'do you do with your mistakes?'

The preacher replied, 'Same as you. Not long since, I meant to say that the devil was the father of all liars, but I made a mistake and said the father of lawyers. Figured the mistake was so small, I let it go.'

Mrs. Lincoln is amused, more so after I reminded her the Writer is also a lawyer. Reminded her again that her son and myself are partners in law. This pleases her more. She enjoys a respite, generally entertained by my stories of our law office. I cannot relate an anecdote that does not fail to amuse Mrs. L. I speak of Abe's vast void of clerical ability—she laughs; I relate that our office gathered filthy sustenance from herbal life sprouting from floor cracks—she laughs; that her grandsons were always welcome with Abe when not in school, and could act as monkeys in his presence—she laughs until I am excused for her relief.

When I return to her bedside Mrs. Lincoln begs my pardon that she lay fully prone. I insist on her comfort. She continued:

"Turns out Abe was waiting on a certain young woman from Lexington, in Kaintuck, to drop her bags at the train station in Springfield. She come to live with her sister. Sister's name escapes me, but as Abe tell it, Mary Todd's sister and the sister's husband were the right fine center of it all, for anyone that was right and fine in Springfield. Abe said he wanted to dance with Mary in the worst way. He tell me about them fancy gowns, best as a man can. I reckon it like I was back in Liztown, afore I settled on a certain Daniel Johnston. I'd a worn them gowns iffin I hadn't settled for a certain Daniel Johnston.

"Abe was nearly thirty, I s'pose, round about the time he first seen Mary Todd. She was almost a spinster at twenty-two years. Abe said she had her light chestnut hair and posh, smooth skin. As Abe tells it, seems most enchanting for my boy were her eyes. Said they were as blue as the sky round sunrise, nary a cloud. Her eyes pierce him like that. All the voting and speeches were right fine, but this was news his Mama was a waiting for. I was plumb tickled when Abe told me she's fond of poetry and could speak French like she was born there. I knew then she was the one he was waiting for. Abe and I grinned over it when he told me the reason Mary Todd showed her face in Springfield, Illinois, back then. Was because she couldn't get on with her stepmother. I teased him some how hard us stepmamas is to get on with."

Author's Note: I speak truthfully of Mary Todd. She was indeed dashing, handsome cultured, graceful and dignified. I dare not sully precious time speaking of Mrs. L's daughter-in-law who was also a truly sarcastic, haughty, and caustic aristocrat. In spite of it, because of it, she became the belle of the town, leading the young men on a merry dance. Not the least of whom was Stephen Douglas. I delight Mrs. L. with Mary Todd's decline of Douglas' jestful proposal of marriage to her. Of herself, she stated, 'Mary Todd wished to marry a President, and so chooses Mr. Abraham Lincoln.' This pleases Mrs. Lincoln vastly. The ever piercing wit and tongue, forked tongue, of Mary Todd. The Todd family was friends and neighbors of Henry Clay in Lexington. The significance was not lost on Mrs. Lincoln. She continues:

"Word come around Christmas, Abe and Mary were engaged. No bliss in it, Abe show up at my door one day reduced and emaciated, could barely speak above a whisper. Took to his bed for a week. Lord a-Mighty, my boy was under a dark cloud for a time. I feed him as much as he could stomach. Spoke to the chillern that were fond of Uncle Abe, saying he was sick and need his Mama's time for now. They were respecting a course. I set by him days gone by, feeling nearly as low down.

"My boy was a felled tree in the woods. I'd speak to Abe when he was recepting of it, but I mostly just held his hand while he rested his mind. We begun to speak on it. Trying, as any Mama might, I explain what mostly can't be explained. Abe prefer the mind. He got through it. Him and Mary got through it. The day come when Abe was purt proud to show me his wedding ring carved, 'Love is eternal.'

"No more than an elephant would a skeeter, Abe never noticed Mary's pestering. He'd just take hold of her hand, or pat her on the shoulder, and she'd quiet down. You bet, Mary was a good woman or Abe never would a loved her like he done. She didn't have nothing personal against us kinfolks, but I reckon she figured we wouldn't help Abe's chances none.

"Mary was smart and high feeling about Abe. When they were fust married she'd toss her head way up in the air like a blood colt, and tell us what a big man Abe was going to be. I know'd afore she did, course I didn't say as much. The chillern enjoyed laughing over Mary's pride in him, for when a feller's as honest as Abe was, they said it generally stands in the way of his gittin on in the world. He purt nigh always got the worst of a trade. And then he didn't look for greatness. He looked just like the rest of us, only some homelier. Kind of common and neighborly, not a bit stuck-up. You just naturally liked to set and visit with Abe.

"Things keep on, one year to the next. Run myself up to twenty-three granbabies crawling, yippin and running in and out my door. Soon enough them babies was borning—arms full a more babies still.

"Abe come for a visit on his way to Washington City to be in the U.S. Congress. Come time for Tommy to fess up that all his foolishness saying Abe was reaching too far. Stubborn man Tommy. He mostly grumble and grouse his way to expressing pride in his boy. Natural as he was prone, Abe took it. They part uneasy.

"I'd go to market round the square in Charleston. Seen folks, strangers to me, come to find out I was Abe's mama. He wasn't popular them days, Abe wasn't what he is today and then a few. Bolder ones try to make their business with me. I send them grinning off their own way when I tell them how politics is like an old woman's dance, short and sweet. That's what Abe reckon I do.

He spent most his time in Washington City arguing about warring with Mexico. He wasn't for it, seemed like a fib to him why we were there, and he wasn't for that. Saying too that taking on new lands was poison. Seen ahead, as Abe done, to a time when them territories would want to become states in the Union, and the question was up for fighting every time if they were coming in Free or Slave. Folks forgot what we been through with Missouri a ways back. Abe seen it, but couldn't do nothing 'cept to face the voters like he was against the soldiers. Naturally he didn't get back to Washington City. Abe was done-for, while his tavern mate Stephen Douglas was the feathered rooster of the barnyard, crowing he was to be President. Little Doug we called him, half as tall as Abe but his head was twice the size of Abe's. Most repugnantly handsome features, them two! They cut quite a pair.

"Abe was done for alright, that's what folks said back then. He stood for right iffin he must lose for it. The Good Lord set his mallet down."

GOOD THING THEY DID

Tell Father

to remember to call upon, and confide in,

our great, and good, and merciful Maker;

who will not turn away from him

in any extremity.

He notes the fall of a sparrow,

and numbers the hairs of our heads;

and He will not forget the dying man,

who puts his trust in Him.

Say to Father that if we could meet now,

it is doubtful

whether it would not be

more painful than pleasant.

7

More Painful than Pleasant

"Tommy Lincoln lived to fire his yarns soon after he took in a traveler, as Tommy was inclined for most any but the slave catchers. He send them on their way in the cold and rain with no further talk at all. For all others, we'd feed 'em up at the table with how-do's and fun with the news from their other stops. We'd set as we are now and have our yarns. Soon as Tommy would find himself his moment, the slightest quiet, I figure to hear these words, 'It wasn't much long after General George sent his boys home that my Pa lit out west for Kaintuck to claim the land given to him in return for his service.' Tommy'd let that set a minute afore he'd follow with, 'Wasn't much longer after that when my Pa was shot dead in his field and this here skull of mine was an arm's distance from a screaming mad Injin and his tomahawk.'"

"I seen it for all types, Tommy have the most weary traveler this wilderness can produce, soon find himself drawing closer, eager for Tommy's next words. After the rightful pause he was off now, sure as sunrise. Got plenty a travelers that final stretch the Lincolns were in Kaintuck, living on the old Cumberland Road. A regular frontier parade of soldiers and peddlers, slaves and slavers too, come long the Lincoln farm between bigger places like Nashville and Louisville. Not as much crowd on the clearing. Once Tommy fire this yarn at the new neighbors he generally went hungry for someone new.

"Tommy said his Pa was a faithful Quaker, believe in the goodness a man. Tommy's Pa's name was Abraham Lincoln. No wonder then that his grandson and namesake may got some a his blood in his veins! My days are full a driving away tearing thoughts how they were both killed for it.

"Tommy take a full breath in now as he fire away with his yarn , how them Lincolns were out in the clearing with the oxen hauling logs down to the crick. Tommy went along, but he wasn't much help, for he was only six. Young as he was, he certainly remember what happened that day like it was only yesterday. He said it come like a bolt out of the blue. He seen his father drop like he was shot. Tommy was fond to stretch some here til he said, 'For he was shot!' Folks were leaned in fully by now while Tommy was glowing like embers. Said next how he heard the crackle of a rifle and saw a puff of smoke floating out of the bushes. It was then he heard his oldest brother Mord gasp, 'Injins!' and make quick for the house to get his gun. Josiah, another a Tommy's brothers, he starts off in the opposite direction to the Beargrass Fort. Tommy would add for certain right about this portion, 'Us Lincoln boys scattered like a brood of young turkeys, striking for cover when the oldest one is shot.'

"Then come the part of his yarn Tommy seem to savor the most. As he said, he know'd he should run as he seen his older brothers striking for cover, but stood aside his Pa as he was shot, and he kneeled aside him. His heart was such, he could not leave him. While he was crouched there, staring like the oxen not knowing what to do, a big Injin come out of the brush with a gleaming knife in his hand. Tommy know'd what he was going to do, scalp the father that lay shot aside him! Tommy, all of six, braced up to the Injin to keep him away. That Injin just laughed, admire the boy's spirit some, I reckon, and pick him up like he was baby. Set him down on a sawlog. At last, he could commence his scalping.

"About now I'm afeared the weary traveler may never sleep again with what Tommy done for them with his yarn. He keep on then how there was another crack of a rifle and just like that the big Injin drops, and Tommy show em just how he wiggled and squirmed round afore he bit the dust. Iffin his crowd was big enough, Tommy would sound off the blood-curdling yells that come from the lot of Injins who jump out of the bushes brandishing their tomahawks and scalping knives. Tommy finally run for the house with them Injins after him. Just as one close on him with his tomahawk raised to brain little Tommy, "Crack!" Mord fetches him down. That repeat itself three more times as Tommy show on his neck just where he could feel the breath of the next yelping Injin, up till he flung himself through the doorway of the Lincoln cabin and they lock up fast behind!

"Troubles were far from concluded. Mord could cover the front of the house with his rifle but the backside had no opening. Sure enough some of them Injins sneaked around behind the house and it wasn't long till Tommy could smell smoke. He said his Mama took his hand, and grabbed the hands of his weeping sisters, and command them all to sing, "Rock of Ages." So they begun when Josiah comes back with a posse of Soldier from Beargrass. Them Injuns were run off, drove off the livestock as they went, but the Lincolns I reckon were happy not to be cooking just then.' Tommy Lincoln was sure to be beaming like noonday sun right then."

Mrs. Lincoln rested her eyes until a lad of perhaps five years, one of Mrs. Lincoln's great-grandchildren, I presume, entered the cabin as the waning sun stretched shadows across the emerald green rag rug. His stated purpose was to request his Granmarm join him on the footpath, as the children had prepared something special. Colonel Chapman offered the old lady his arm but she reached out to the Writer. She grasped my arm with surprising strength, nearly supporting me, contrary to the original proposition. Mrs. L. seemed delighted with the surprise and eager to see it revealed. Thus supported, we walked slowly out. Colonel Chapman followed with her rocking chair, which he held for her at the head of the path. In the yard a dozen boys and girls of various ages stood in a double line, facing each other. As Sarah settled in her chair, the children began clapping hands and the tallest of the boys called out the steps. It was a rousing display. When it was done, Sarah laughed and applauded and beckoned the children to come to her.

"Now, you all go on help your Mama's," she instructed them. "Git the vittels ready. If vittels is set, well then help somewheres else. Be good chillern for your Mamas. Now git!" She playfully sent them off again, before settling back into her chair, in no hurry to resume.

"Praire sunset." Mrs. Lincoln took time now to gather herself. "The day begs its peace." After more time still she added, "This life is cumbersome, Billy. I was plenty sure the Good Lord still had purpose for this old bag a bones from the clearing." Borrowing from her husband's love of yarn, she added after a considered pause, "Maybe just enough to kill me."

Mrs. Lincoln rocked back and forth for a several minutes, eyes alert, fixed on the horizon. She resumed:

"Abe's wedding stir trouble with a long spoon. Tommy took it sour Abe didn't have us Lincolns invited. Whip up all the Grigsby troubles again, only this time it was Abe who done it. Chillern were no help neither, the way they went to stoking Tommy's fire. Was a preferred topic. Can't say as I wouldn't a made more noise than a loose mule in a tin barn had I been asked. Abe know'd best, and that was always enough for a blame fool such as me. Them gowns must a been something, Billy."

Here I explained Mr. L's wedding was thrown together with haste. It was a small crowd of thirty guests, if that, married in the dining room of a friend's home. The best man was informed of his honor on the very day of the wedding. Mrs. L. amused by this, and greatly comforted. She continued:

"Abe was prone to say, 'Sorrow come to us all.' Abe and Mary done their suffering. Their little boy Eddie was buried when he was but four years old. Mary was a tender soul. I know'd burying her babe wrung her dry. There come a stretch when it seem those of us that were left still standing were wrung dry as well. Chickens today, feathers tomorrow. That's what my Mama was fond of saying. And so it was that Squire pass suddenly, leaving Tildy a widow with eight mouths to feed. My sweet Betsy was finally taken into Loving Arms after years of suffering. Then come Tommy to fall ill. I didn't see for him rising from the bed again neither but dog me if I do, Billy! Tommy Lincoln never was one to pick a fight with, and he come back! My guess is a passel of screaming chillern chase him right out of his bed.

"Next come John D.'s wife. Mary was daylong kin with me, being nearby as she was. Me and Mary were bonded for all time as we both fall for the same special kind a bushy haired, princely Johnston boy. Finely dressed kind, good for dancing, and devil's bait for sparking. Not men for much else. I done my best to look after Mary as she begun to see the jail her life become with my Johnny, just as I seen years afore for myself with Johnny's Pa. Mary and me done our share a yelping and thrashing on it afore we seen we were stuck. Ventually tuckered ourselves out and just done our best tending to our little seeds. She was one of mine now.

"For a time Johnny, Mary, Tildy and me, we done our best while Denny was in Charleston cobbling and tinkering to keep up for Betsy's chillern. Tommy was mostly done for working, setting a date on when that day come was sure fire to be a lively scrap! We had plenty of hard scrabbling to git a living. From dawn to dusk and then by candlelight, seem I was all feed, spin, seed, water, weave, sew, and soap. Always soaping something, kittles and pans, chillern, floor.

"I can see now just like it was yesterday when Mary showed me the palm of her hand. Both of us seen it right then for bad sick, her thumb lay flat like. Wasn't no way a knowing it was just the beginning. Mary just begun to wither away, like the Good Lord done reached inside and begun pulling her out. She went to fewer than bones, couldn't hardly move, and then she couldn't move a'tall. I think on it, Billy, how a woman who couldn't move none was the strongest I ever seen. Course Johnny plagueing her at first, as he was having to move himself more than he care to, and the chillern couldn't a known any better, and Mary just grin her way on and on best she could, till the day come. Mary is in heaven I have no doubt. Then as now, I was still very much of this earth, and I was a Mama again for more chillern still, just as it once was, 'ceptin for the gray and brittle hair beneath my bonnet.

"John D. was off like a bunny for a child bride. Seem like poor Mary hardly been laid to rest when Johnny lit out for Missouri to see the newest land of milk and honey. Reckon he suit himself soon as he come upon a parcel so fine there'd be no need to plow it, then gone on to seed and harvest itself. Tildy and me took on his chillern, on loan, John D. promising to return. That was the last promise John D. broke, as he up and died. Tildy and I were more sisters like, though she still find her way to her Mama's shoulder, tearing up like she did when she was a young'un, all torn up over a corncob doll. Now her problems were real—men and money.

"Them twenty-three chillern were generally walking with their chin high like that Liztown sparker by name of Sally Bush. Ages somewheres betwixt young enough for young trouble and old enough for old trouble. It was too much for Tommy, he took ill, sure he was fixin' to pass. Col. Chapman's wife, Harriett, got the news to Abe right quick that Tommy was wishing to see him. Few days later she got a letter from Abe saying that iffin it's his Pa's time, our Maker is a merciful one, and notes when one sparrow falls and knows even the hairs on our head, and would surely recognize a dying man who put trust in Him. He said more still, wound Tommy something fierce, said things might be more painful than pleasant were they to see each other.

"He leave Tommy to die like that and don't even attend his funeral. If ever I was tested by Abe it was then. Lord a-Mighty, I ached every way I found I could, and come up with a few new ones that day we lay Tommy to rest without Abe present. My only comfort, Billy, was Tommy finally released the grip between them. Tommy Lincoln was reunited with the Pa he searched the world over for, the man he name his boy after, and the man who didn't live to school his son what a Pa done. Seem Tommy and Abe were bound to be raw, not the last father and son bent on scrapping.

"Would a meant a hoot to Tommy if he'd lived to know Abe name his next boy Thomas. Abe seen it after all it, after my Tommy was in the ground. Abe finally seen his Pa for his goodness. Reckon kinfolks counted for more in early days. I'm just tired everybody runs Grandfather Lincoln down. Tommy would a got something ahead if he hadn't been so generous. He had the old Virginia notion of hospitality, liked to see people sit up to the table and eat hearty, and there were always a plenty of relations willing to pull up a chair! Abe got his honesty from Tommy, and his clean notions of living and his kind heart and high morals. Jabbers may jab Tommy was shiftless iffin they please, don't change what I know'd, Tommy was kind and loving, and kept his word, and always paid his way, and never turned a dog from his door. You couldn't say that of every man, not even today, when men are decenter than they used to be.

"I know Tommy seen it in Heaven, Abe naming his boy Thomas after him. Would a been fine had he been setting right where you are, Billy, upon hearing word Abe named his boy Thomas. Them two were a pair, Tommy and Abe, yearning for Nancy still. She'd had them bound together as I could not." Here Mrs. L. weeps.

"Folks everyday strife, plentiful as it was, reach the Good Lord who was plumb distracted. The troubles were here now, the first jolts come when Stephen Douglas pass Kansas-Nebraska and soon enough John Brown was decapitating slavers in Bleeding Kansas. There wasn't no room for worse—worse was now, so we fools figured back then. I seen so much heartache, Billy, it's a wonder why I seem chosen to survive it. Mostly nothing left to be wrung out no more, so I enjoy them chillern and their sunset prancing. The comfort of a kitchen, and seeing them little ones in your shadow with their big eyes and big questions, knowing their times ahead afore they do, knowing just how much aggravation they were in for. This, Billy, is where my hours are best as can be since..."

By the manner in which Mrs. L. trailed off, there was no purpose in vocalizing the completion of her thought; it was well known to the Writer. She did, even so, "The best as can be after Abe was gone." She continued:

"Just as I expect my heart to burst open for all to fret, certain as a soul can be that I couldn't take no more, it was gonna be war now. My kin in Kaintuck were gonna kill my Indianny and Illinois kin, who were gonna kill em back! Madness all around!

"Here now The Almighty made His way on His errand to the gawkiest boy who ever obstructed my view. The Lord said to Abraham, 'I will make you into a great nation.'

"Abe know'd it from all them nights back, reading aloud by the fire light as he did from Matthew, Mark, and Luke, saying many a time that a house divided against itself can't stand. The time had come to settle it."

Mr. Lincoln asks you to elect him
to The United States Senate today
solely because he can slander me.
Has he given any other reason?
Has he avowed
what he was desirous to do in Congress
on any one question?
He desires to ride into office
not upon his own merits,
not upon the merits
and soundness of his principles,
but upon his success
in fastening a state slander upon me.

8

He Desires To Ride Into Office

Twilight deepened. The first night wind passed right through Mrs. Lincoln, "put a chill on my gizzards," the dear lady maintained, wishes to return to the cabin. Colonel Chapman helped her rise. Writer offered his arm, which seemed to please her. Tildy greeted us as we reentered the cabin home, warmed her Mama's face with her hands, and pulled Mrs. L.'s shawl up over her shoulders, ruffling the excess snugly around her neck. Wrapping her arms around her Mama's torso, Tildy lowered Mrs. Lincoln slowly into her rocking chair, a scant few feet in front of the glowing hearth. Mrs. L. looked off with a vacancy I had not seen since early in my visit, her vitality following the setting sun.

Before I could concern myself with probabilities our afternoon together would conclude before her story's end, Mrs. L. stirs, as though acknowledging there was more work to be done, likely not her first doze upended by such thoughts. She resumed:

"Abe done a lot of traveling court back then, running around the countryside settling up for folks. Nothing to do with the evening but to set around the tavern stove firing yarns. Nobody could beat Abe at it. He would just slap his hands on his knees and jump up and turn around and then set down, laughing fit to kill when someone fire a good yarn at his ear. Abe said Old Judge Davis was the boss of the lot, and the Judge wasn't one for starting up on their sessions til Abe come along, as he'd say to anyone who was for listening, 'Where's Abe?' Course, the Judge might say it like, 'Where's Lincoln?' and somebody would go and fetch my boy, Lincoln.

"I saw Abe every year or two, when his lawyering brung him to Charleston. We would set by the hearth by the hour while he fire his yarns and let me ask him all the questions I could think of bout his boys and Mrs. Lincoln. I'd set my hand on his, never once looking away from his face. My son look a man a real honor and distinction. My heart ache with pride to hear him speak on his times, riding the circuit along with some right smart lawyers. Abe said he know'd Stephen Douglas from the sessions they have while passing the hours set around them tavern stoves. Abe said he was hell-fire bent to lock horns with the man someday.

"I'm not much for poly'tics myself, Billy. I know'd Abe's heart. If Abe say it, then that's how it was for me. Rest of them round the square in Charleston, they were running out of words. Fists begun to clench and Lord a-Mighty—the thunder turn to storm. Folks were scared a what come next. Abe and Little Doug finally face off on it when they run for Senate.

"Abe make his point by likening slavery to a poison snake that come crawling along the road. Abe said we musn't kill it straight off, iffin it keep to its business. If that poison snake was in the bed of a neighbor's chillern, then it be for him to figure it out. The fight come when the neighbor try to put the snake in our chillern's beds. Abe said he was wishing to discuss it with Little Doug, but the big bug was to afraid tho face the facts. When Little Doug refuse to debate Abe, all them newspapers come out fitting him into a coward's suit. It got the best of him, and so they begun meeting all over Illinois. Day before they come into Charleston, Chapman come with his buggy for me. Said there wasn't gonna be time for Abe to come see me here, so I was to stay the night with Harriet, off the city square.

"Was warmer than I like for traveling, much the same time a year as now. I prefer to be still in such heat. Can't be still for too long though or I might just stop moving! Chapman took me into Charleston, after we see the clearing at the fairground where Abe would have his words with Little Doug. Was a fresh platform built, just like they were having a camp meeting, split logs turned flat-side up for setting on, row after row. I ain't never seen so many rows, even when it seem half a Kaintuck was there.

"Chapman said there would be folks standing behind them split logs for as far as my eyes could see. I figured my dearest grandson was stretching the matter some. As we approached Charleston, where Chapman lived with Harriet, I seen he may a spoke truth somehows.

"Billy, I never seen none like it, afore or since. Dog my hide if there weren't folks of all walks heared and seen all round, full mile still from Charleston. There were folks seeming to appear in every bit of my view. Right then people were paying no attention to an old woman riding along in a buggy. Town was near all get out for Abe and Little Doug. Folks were spilling out of the front of hotels and others were offering their homes if they were all for the same man. They were most jolly to each other, seem, the day before. The square was decorated with all kinds a red, white and blue, with flags and drapes, and banners so big they hung from one building to the next. Biggest of all hung from the courthouse to a building on the west side of the square, must a been eighty feet, with a picture of Abe looking like a boy again, standing in a wagon driving an ox team. Harriet said it read, 'Old Abe Thirty Years Ago.' Ate a nice meal at Harriet's that evening. They give up their feather bed to creeky old Granmarm Lincoln. I try my best not to think on the big-eyed time I was to have that next day.

"I know'd long ago what the Lord set out for Abe. Couldn't picture it none back then. I couldn't a seen it to that very day, til I seen it. Just bedlam the whole gathering was. Little Doug was coming in by the north road, so they send Abe by the old south road to keep the fighting to what they could keep it to. Day was hot, right from dawn it seemed. Chillern saved a place for me so I could rest in the house til they heard a ruckus coming. Lad come to fetch me and drag me off, brung a brother or two for feeble me. Little hands in mine always gives me spring, like they were giving me some a their young through their tiny fingertips. He drug me to the spot alongside the south road. I seen a float drawn by eight horses, decorated with white muslin and silk wildflowers, carrying thirty-two girls in white dresses and blue velvet caps. I know there were thirty-two because Harriet told me there was a girl for each state. She said each girl carried a silver star and was wearing a banner with the name of their state in the Union on it. Was another girl, riding a white horse. She wore a banner for Kansas while holding a flag of sorts. Harriet said it read, "I will Be Free."

"Soon enough word run through the crowd that Abe was coming round soon. I stayed right where I was setting, although it was hot and my heart was thumping in my chest like a loose mule. I stood when Chapman said he could see Abe on top of a grand carriage. I could not make out one from the other just yet. Took some time for me to fix my eyes on Abe, and I when I done it I nearly went right home to get cooking! He look too much like the skeleton I found in the wilderness all them years ago, 'ceptin he was handsome as could be in his black suit and tall hat. Looked tired. Lord a-Mighty, I was wishing I could just bring him back home with me for a few days. I know'd what Abe needed, all the way to a hard ache in my heart. He come even closer and I look round me at the hysteria, as if a fire was offin somewheres. Them folks were seeing Abe as he was, it come off him, seeing him up there. They know'd Abe's heart, just meeting his eyes. The Lord had no place for my aches with what He was having Abe to do. So it must be, Billy. So it must be.

"Abe was waving and smiling for all them people dumbstruck for his attention, knowing he carry their hopes to end slavery, just as I know'd it back when he come home from New Orleans. His carriage amble its way upon us, where Abe stood up and speak to his driver. Driver pulled in the reins and begun barking up ahead for the others to stop else the whole parade come apart, which got them barking up ahead a them, and on up the line. Floats behind Abe had to stop a course, and the whole parade come to a halt with no one but Abe figuring what was to be.

"Folks were cheering themselves purple when Abe stood up in his carriage. He wave them on with great courtesy, not lingering in my view as he disappear into the swarm. I had to set just then with the heat and all; it become too much. There was quite a stir. Folks were waving like wheat, so abundant, and the screams were piercing to a deaf old woman such as myself! I seen the crowd begun to part like Moses scooting off from the Pharaoh. I didn't even have time to feel a plumb bit embarrassed, as I am now figuring back on it, to have all them people looking my way. Some folk were looking right on me as I never cared for from a stranger, but most were looking away from me, peering off in the opposite direction, whooping and a hollering as though the lot of them dropped a rock on their foot. I was too old for all this excitement; I recall thinking I might just keel over.

"Round then the crowd cleared aside some, and right in front of me, standing afore a hooting wild crowd, was my son. Brung all them people to their toes fetching a gander at him. There he was, Abraham Lincoln. He stood there with eyes for me only. Somehow, for all the percular challenge the Good Lord saddle him with for looks, he growed into a man to set your eyes on with comfort. His suit was rumpled up and dusty of course. Cared nothing for clothes and fashion cut no figure with him, nor color, nor stuff, nor material. Abe was careless about these things.

"It happened so fast, too fast. He climbed down off that wagon and come right to me and said, 'Thanks for coming, Ma.' He give me a big kiss on the cheek and told me he was glad I was there. Knowing it was so, he said, was gonna help him a lot. That was about all we could manage with all them people waiting, 'ceptin to promise to see me after it was all over. I could not take in my breath long after Abe walked off through all them cheering folks, and climb back up into his carriage. He was moving with the parade afore I could freely breath again.

"Round noon when we pick up and head off for the fairgrounds clearing. Chapman was weaving his buggy in and out amongst folks to get to me. I become more than just another old lady in a bonnet, I become Abraham Lincoln's mama. Folk I ain't ever seen afore or since sprung on me that day to say nice things about Abe, which wasn't much a problem til we come closer to the clearing and begun to encounter Little Doug's folks. What we seen the day afore wasn't half a what was coming in on wagon load. People as far as I could see. All of them coming to see Abe and Little Doug get back around the tavern stove to argue slavery.

"Ammunition and whiskey were enormously cheap it seem, and the crowd was fixin' to settle it themselves. All the jolly cooked off yesterday. Today it seem as soon as one battle was over, some other man would take it up. I was taunted by some that were in for Little Doug, them that were leaving their good sense in a whiskey barrel. The big platform I seen the day afore was an island barely visible in a restless sea, so great was the gathering. Above this swarm a people were giant banners with words on them. Harriet read all the signs a waving above the crowd a folks to us:

THIS GOVERNMENT MADE FOR WHITE MEN – DOUGLAS FOR LIFE!
ABE THE GIANT KILLER
I LIKE THIS'N THAT HARRIET READ TO ME: OUR GIRLS LINK-ON TO
LINCOLN. THEIR MOTHERS WERE FOR CLAY

"Chapman took me right up to them split log benches where Tildy was setting. Between the folk we seen yesterday spilling out of every doorway, and all them wagonloads from the morning, people were a hundred and more deep standing in all directions, and dressed for gathering. Behind them a ways off were more still, standing in their wagons. Never seen anything like it afore or since, the stage was done up in red white and blue drapes. Abe sat up there with a few other men. I never once set eyes on Little Doug afore so Chapman pointed him out to me.

"Lord a-Mighty! I was ready to turn around right then, for he seemed cunning and give a sense that he know'd what to do. Appeared to me he had a big head generally, and a face with the expression of a man who done swallered something sour. But his hair was fancy as any woman's and his eyebrows were massive. By the very looks of him, strong looking jaw, here was a lion, master of himself and of others. He was dressed to a T in a lavender check suit. Made a silk it seemed. By then Abe and his suit were wilted and he looked a bit rough and uncouth. My poor boy. I felt sorry for him as the two stood up to greet the crowd afore they went to yippin at each other like hounds frisky for a hunt.

"Abe spoke first while Little Doug set and took it. Abe's voice was clear without being strong. Time Abe was done it was Little Doug stepping up to talk. Now I felt sorry for him, seeing as how the way Abe'd said it there didn't seem to be no other way. Little Doug done his best a course, saying states should settle their slaving preferences like they were squatters, with squatters' rights. Spoke a the Kansas-Nebraska Act, and some lavender suit nonsense about Popular Sovereignty. Didn't seem none too popular with the folks that were assembled. Abe said Little Doug's arguments were as thin as soup made from the shadow of a pigeon that starved to death.

"Crowd was a whooping and hollering then, just roaring with laughter. Was the show they come for and Abe was given it to them! But then he quiet us all down, make it still, and get everbody's full attention. I seen Little Doug up there, waiting his chance as Abe made his points. His body sort a slumped whilst Abe deliver his thumping. You'd a thought we were gonna hang him on that stage stead a let him speak. Abe turn serious and we were all set still.

"He raised his hand in the air, finger to a point, and he said to the hushed crowd, 'Slavery. That is the real issue and would be, after our poor tongues shall be silent. That it was the eternal struggle between two principles that stood face-to-face since the beginning of time—right and wrong!' Abe said some other things I was a bit surprised by, as for Negros being jurors. I meant to ask him about later. Course I could not. So many unasked questions, Billy.

"Come a time in the speaking when Abe become angry. Abe never could tolerate foolishness well. Little Doug said Abe voted not to supply our soldiers during the warring with Mexico back when Abe was in the Congress. Abe stopped the Little Giant right then, couldn't have that for people's ears for the love of truth. So Abe went and plucked a man out a the crowd, a man who was there in Washington City with Abe. Democrat too, I believe. (Writer confirms, it was Democratic Congressman, Orlando B. Ficklin). He was a larger man and the crowd seen Abe's strength as he brung that man up to the stage. When he got him there, Abe asked him to speak how Abe voted when it come to supplying our troops. Well sir, the man said right then how Abe done so, making Douglas' words false. Folks were a whooping ever which way, veins bulging from their necks for what Abe done to Little Doug.

"For the longest time Illinois shine on Douglas, he was our great man. He knew all the big bugs all over the country and sort a looked and talked like he was one of them. Abe was such that even the real old-fashioned Jackson Democrats voted for him, for they liked him and how he was so all-fired smart, mostly from the stories he tell. People know'd goodness off him strong as sugar sap set to boil in the backwoods of Kaintuck.

"There were more rallies after they speak themselves quiet. Democrats in the Courthouse, Republicans at the Square. Abe came to Chapman's house just as soon as he could. Between the yarns he fire and the jokes, I done my best to feed him hearty food while he set jack-knifed in a chair, feet propped against the wall higher than his head. Chillern of all ages gathered round Abe, and he wasn't too shy to fun with them while Denny was speeching, to Abe's great amusement, about how he run off to see Little Doug after we seen Abe that morning at the parade. Denny said there was a painted sign above the crowd that showed Abe holding a club and just about to slay the Little Giant. So Douglas stuck his big gray hat outta the carriage and said he'd get out of the procession if he couldn't be treated with respect! Folks just laughed mostly, and Little Doug tucked himself back in and keep on a riding.

"Round about then a local band of supporters come by to serenade Abe. He said they were gonna keep up till he spoke, so he promised to return soon as he satisfied them with a few words. Billy, I have the newspaper writing if you wish to scrawl his words. I believe it's time for me to tend to my needs."

Writer assures Mrs. Lincoln that he does indeed wish to copy the newspaper article. She called to her granddaughter to assist her to the privy.

"Upon her return, Mrs. L. requested I read the article to her, saying, "It always does my heart good to hear it." And so, Writer was happy to oblige and read those granite-carved words to the dear lady:

"A house divided against itself cannot stand. I believe this government cannot endure, permanently half slave and half free. I do not expect the Union to be dissolved -- I do not expect the house to fall -- but I do expect it will cease to be divided. It will become all one thing or all the other.

Either the opponents of slavery will arrest the further spread of it, and place it where the public mind shall rest in the belief that it is in the course of ultimate extinction; or its advocates will push it forward, till it shall become alike lawful in all the States, old as well as new -- North as well as South.

Two years ago the Republicans of the nation mustered over thirteen hundred thousand strong. We did this under the single impulse of resistance to a common danger, with every external circumstance against us. Of strange, discordant, and even, hostile elements, we gathered from the four winds, and formed and fought the battle through, under the constant hot fire of a disciplined, proud, and pampered enemy.

Did we brave all then to falter now? — now — when that same enemy is wavering, dissevered and belligerent? The result is not doubtful. We shall not fail — if we stand firm, we shall not fail.

Wise councils may accelerate or mistakes delay it, but, sooner or later the victory is sure to come.

Friends, it would be my great honor to greet each and every one of you. I invite you all for a gathering on the square at nine tonight. Until then I wish to be left with family.'

With that, Abe returned inside the residence of Augustus and Harriet Chapman.

Mrs. Lincoln returned soon after the above transcription was completed. She took up her story again:

"Abe come back that night after the last rally finally ended, and with the little ones around me, one of my grown babes climb in too, scooching a couple of the tots aside so he could lay next to his Mama. I fear I would cut a deal with the Devil, Billy, to have them moments back again.

"I told Abe how I weep sometimes when I think of his little Eddie being gone. Abe let out his grief with his Mama, just as I know'd he was wishing to do. Done my all to seep up his tears like them sponges he brung from New Orleans. After a while he moved his weeping on to his Mama and Sairy. My boy had a heavy heart. There he was again, curled up aside his Mama, and soon enough he breathe deep. He rested his head on my shoulder for a peace that was too short, a peace he didn't git near enough. Railroad was to depart at four the next morning. I slept not a'tall, instead clinging to every minute left to breathe his scent and hold it, and feel his slow and steady breath, and squeeze my son tight as I could, so long as I didn't stir him awake. Abe's friend, a Mr. Whitney I recall, tapped on Chapman's door to fetch Abe. Durn near impossible for me to let go of him, but the time had come for it.

"Wasn't enough for Abe to win the arguing that time. Little Doug went back to the Senate. The rest seen how Abe made his way against their Little Giant, and they were going to lean on it when the time come to pick their man for President two years later. Right make might, Abe went on to say on behalf of the Good Lord Himself. I did not want Abe to run for President — did not want him Elected — was afraid somehow or other. I felt it in my heart that something would happen to him."

I saw him every year or two.

He was here

after he was elected

President of the U.S.

(Here the old lady stopped,

turned around and cried —

wiped her eyes

and then proceeded.)

Here the Old Lady Stopped

Writer notes the President-Elect left Springfield, Illinois, twice over the ten month span from his dark horse nomination to his departure as future President. He travelled to Chicago to introduce himself to his Vice President, Sen. Hannibal Hamlin of Maine. Mr. Lincoln's final destination was this very hearthside. Col. Augustus H. Chapman, who stands in our presence, was his escort that day from Charleston Station to Goosenest Prairie.

Herein is the deposition of Colonel. Augustus H. Chapman, Husband of Harriet Hanks Chapman, the maternal granddaughter of Sarah Bush Lincoln. He began:

"It was evening when Abe arrived at the Charleston Depot. Folks put out in the cold to glimpse at him. Seemed the only way Abe was to get in that night was by freight train. They stopped a ways back from the platform. Quite a site to see the President-Elect ina pea coat and faded plug hat making his way through the long expanse of slush and ice beside the track. His baggage was comprised only of a well-worn carpetbag, quite collapsed. Word of our arrival spread. By the time Abe arrived at his overnight location at Senator Marshall's house on Washington Street, the town's brass band was awaiting us there to serenade him. He wasn't for speeching, more keen to swap stories with friends. Granmarm Lincoln kept the newspaper story if you wish to transcribe it.

Herein the second page Mattoon Weekly Gazette under the heading, Ol' Abe Loose.

Mr. Lincoln, who seems to have made a temporary escape from the office-seeking host at Springfield, passed through this place last Wednesday evening. He came in on the regular evening train from Chicago, and went on the freight to Charleston. Thinking it none of our business what Mr. Lincoln's business in Charleston was, we made no inquiries. The large crowd, made up of all political parties, which collected on the platform, was evidently delighted to see him, and he greeted his old friends as cordially as though he was friend Lincoln and not the most noted personage in the civilized world.

Since writing the above we learned from the papers that Mr. Lincoln was on a visit to his step-mother.

Col. Augustus H. Chapman, continued:

"The curtain was shut behind him so Abe could come home to see his Mama. We were ill at the thought he couldn't attend, with him running the country now. We prayed on it for Granmarm. She begged us off, saying she know'd Abe was too busy for such nonsense as a visit to his foolhead old Mama, but we knew her heart wasn't in it. She pined to see Abe, fretting over and again how she would not see him again. Of course Abe come back. He know'd in his heart he'd a-been a river boatman with some good fortune, if he ain't turn out to be bear grub back in Indiana. Instead he come into the arms of Granmarm Lincoln. Abe was powerful grateful to Granmarm, a fact known to all without even a mention of it, though it seemed to me then he just come back to see his Mama off.

"While we rode along the eight miles from Charleston to Granmarm's, I saw Andrew Allison on horseback, who was naturally bug-eyed at the sight of my passenger. I ask if he would mind scooting ahead of us to give Granmarm news of her impending visitor. Along the way, Mr. Lincoln spoke of his stepmother in the most affectionate manner; said she had been his best friend in the world, and that no son could love a mother more than he loved her. He also told me of the condition of his family at the time his father married his stepmother, and of the change she made in the family, and of the encouragement he received from her.

"As Granmarm's cabin come in to our view Abe spoke of the butterflies gathering in his stomach as he approached her home. Then he mused on the power of unarmed women and spoke of Harriet Beecher Stowe as the woman who made this great war.

"Uncle Abe thanked me for the ride, and spoke kindly of our time together. Took to himself as we slowed and come right up on Granmarm's door. I hear him knock some, asking if his Mama had time for some company. She cried all over him."

Mrs. Lincoln breathes deeply, as though returning to the state in which I found her. With the determination of one who grunted and gashed her way West, she willed her way forward. She spoke:

"Was a knock, as Chapman said. Abe, with his joshing, had me tickled afore he was even inside. Well sir, Abe knocked, asking me if I had time for a visitor. Not a second later the door swung open, slow like. I know'd Abe was still funning with me some, and then he poke round the door and reveal himself in the firelight. Lord a-Mighty, he was too skinny! My boy looked like he ain't slept a minute in a full month, with them charcoal rings around his eyes. But he was handsome as can be in his beard! My rail-thin boy grew a beard to fill out his face, a right fine idea. Abe said a little girl wrote to him and said she reckon Abe'd look smart with a beard. Abe was always one to listen to the loving suggestions of womenfolk. Done him good!

"I was jumpy as a frog on a frypan right about then, and sure nuff my son was stooping down to the side of my chair, just as I set with you now, Billy. I wasn't for words yet. All I could do was wrap my arms round his neck and pull my boy in tight. God is loving and kind, steeped strong in tender mercy. I cried with Abe, us'n pulled tight. It was Grace itself that my boy made it back. I wasn't in no hurry to let go, and Abe wasn't for being let go, so we set like that, like we were simple, crying and laughing and we ain't said nary a word yet, neither one of us."

Mrs. Lincoln's lungs require deep expulsions; she is winded now. Rests.

Col. A.H. Chapman, Continued:

"Abe was of the highest spirits on his ride to Goosenest Prairie. Recounted his day's journey from Springfield with great delight, starting with him slipping out his home at dawn of the morning prior, he crossed to the east side of the street, into the shadows of a rising sun. Took great pleasure in the plan to escape town undetected, where the streets were shoulder-to-shoulder with office-seekers trying their darndest to find the same one man. Abe come into the side door of the Great Western Railroad Station, a short distance from his Springfield home at Eighth and Jackson, and collar pulled up he skulked up a stair well to the Station Superintendent's Office. An escort, a Mr. Henry Whitney, was inside waiting on him.

Mrs. Lincoln interjected, "See how Abe had it all figured, Billy?"

A.H. Chapman, Cont'd:

"Abe said his mood soured a bit after Whitney read him the news while they waited on the train from the Superintendent's Office. Texas Secession Convention—a hundred sixty-six in favor and seven against. Abe spoke of President Buchanan's comment in one article that the states had 'no right to secede,' while he professed in another that the federal government had 'no right to stop states from seceding.'

"Soon Abe was eager to speak of anything else. Was amused by the faces when he slipped onto the train in Springfield. He said it was as if they seen a ghostly spirit, but once they recovered they were joyous to see their old friend and neighbor. He took the 3:50 Chicago Express, arriving in Mattoon at 5:15. The last eastbound passenger train was not scheduled to leave until 11:35 in the evening. It was then Abe suggested they get on the next freight going east. My first-hand accounts aside, I often tickle myself at the sight of Abe in his plug hat, malnourished, exhausted, mind-a-suffering, setting on a stack of hay aboard a freight train. He may just as well a been a vagrant."

Mrs. Lincoln, it is revealed at the hacking sound of her congested laughter, is following the depositioner, A.H. Chapman.

"The freights were running along the back so Abe stopped short of the platform. As I spoke earlier, he had to walk through ice and snow alongside the tracks. That's when I seen him first. There were maybe a hundred of us, most wanting to set eyes on a President. Abe weaved in and out through the crowd, greeting folks vigorously. More than once I heard him across the platform, 'Lord a-Mighty! So glad to see you!' I took Abe to Sen. Marshall's fine home on the square, where Abe stayed overnight. At first light I took Abe to the west side of the square, to the home of Dennis Hanks, before we departed for Goosenest Prairie."

Mrs. Lincoln requests tea. Tildy is soon to her side, holding the saucer a short distance from the cup embraced with both hands by Mrs. Lincoln. She gulps unabashedly, comfortable in my presence. She returns the cup to the saucer. "My Tildy spiles me with sweet, sweet honey." Mrs. L. licked her lips, continued:

"Abe was frightful skinny; that was all I could speak. Was like I was being choked alive, my throat was so tight. It was then he brung out a box for me, which I refused to open, and plagued Abe generally for such nonsense. Truth of it, I was most tickled that my boy has half the world on the chase for him and here he finds time to select a present and bring it to his half-wit Mama. Just him setting beside a me was a gift unfit for a lady fool enough to grow old on the clearing. Was a fur cape in that box. Sinfully beautiful, which was just right for old Sally Bush!

"Abe and I finally set down, and I look him over while he fire me his yarns. I run my fingers along the lines in his face, trying my best not to make them so long, and so deep. Abe's hair was always a garden in need a weeding and I done my best to put some order to it. What a man my boy become. I told Abe, 'I don't want you to be President.' He was greatly amused by this, reminding me that not many do. Says thirty-nine percent, if we were counting. Round about that time, Abe asks to see Tommy's grave. Tildy dispatched Chapman to fetch his buggy and they were off."

Mrs. L. begs my pardon that she may rest her eyes. Her breathing is soon heavy.

Col. A.H. Chapman, Cont'd:

"Shiloh Cemetery was a mile to the west. Some say Abe, with his own hands, cut the letters "T" and "L" into a small walnut board and placed it at the head of the grave. I state here, with the authority of the one person present, I witnessed no such action. Abe asked me to find out the probable cost of a tombstone for his father's grave. He asked me what the expense might be. I answered that it would not be less than forty dollars, nor more than sixty. Abe said to find out and let him know at Washington, and he would send an inscription he wanted put on it. Abe never furnished me with the inscription for Grandfather Lincoln's headstone, and none was erected on his grave.

"While Abe and I were at Shiloh, word spread that Granmarm was receiving a visitor, and afore long ministers and rail-splitters, folks from every walk of life, began to appear from nowhere. Mr. Osborne dismissed school so his pupils and their teacher could join the growing crowd outside Tildy's home. When Abe returned, he greeted all of them, offering each his hand to shake. Tildy put a nice meal on a table that was no more than planks on sawhorses, run from one end of the house to the other.

"Abe seemed to enjoy it so much that his face was continually lit up with a sunny smile. All were at their ease. Outside, the school children were putting their feet in Abe's shoes, which he'd left by the door, shining on how they stood in the shoes of a President. After dinner Abe stood beside Granmarm while she sat in her chair, his big hand gently rocking her while he rested an elbow of the other arm on the mantelpiece."

Mrs. Lincoln requests Tildy's assistance. She sits up, with some effort she expectorates. She breathes more freely, wishes to continue:

"I said to Abe, 'Here and hereafter, all the things that make us right and worthy must be near you—always. All the good the Savior gave the world was communicated through the Good Book. But for It, we could not know right from wrong.' I asked him to keep it close.

"Abe looked me right in my eyes and told me clear, 'Without the assistance of the Divine Being, I cannot succeed. With that assistance I cannot fail. Trusting in Him who can go with me, and remain with you, Mama, I will keep a Bible on my desk always.' He done it too. Dennis said it was so when he visited Abe in Washington City.

"I feared the time'd come soon for me to say my goodbyes to Abe. Sure enough, I begun to cry and could not stop for all the Lord's Mercy. Just then, Abe asked if I'd be his guest for one more night, join him on his trip back to Charleston. Billy, I sobbed like a fool at just the thought of it. Rode with Abe in the buggy back to Charleston. Abe insisted I wear the fur cape he give me, to which I conceded."

Mrs. L. requests Tildy pat her back. With effort she expectorates, is disappointed by the volume - breathes heavily. "The ride was over much too quickly," she added. Requests rest.

Col. A. H. Chapman took up the story:

"The crowd overflowed two blocks deep around my house. Once again it seemed all of Charleston knew Abe's plans. They pushed and shoved to one side or another to allow the carriage through, generally cheering the President-Elect. Abe waved and tipped his plug hat in both directions as we approached the house. Once fully stopped, he stood and again tipped his hat to the joyous assembled. They hushed, thinking Abe might make a speech but he wasn't for speaking right then, 'cept to say it would be his great honor to greet each and every one of them, invited folks for a town hall reception.

"Abe stepped down from the wagon and weaved his way through the backslappers to reach Granmarm Lincoln on the other side of the carriage. He held his arm up to her so she could steady herself. I heard him say to her, 'I seem to recall you stepping down from a wagon forty-some years ago.' And Granmarm sassed back how Abe looked a little better this time. Once he had Granmarm seated, Abe worked his way to the stage to dispense with the single item of business before he could rejoin the gathering as their returning and departing neighbor. The President-Elect stood on the third step to the stage, chest-high above the crowd. He told folks he knew they wished to hear from him figuring the outlook for the future. But he reckoned it best not speech on it, wishing rather to take each by the hand."

Mrs. Lincoln then interjected, "A few of the bolder women expressed the desire to be able to say they kissed the cheek of the President of the United States.

Imagine that, women fancying to kiss my boy. What fool'd a dreamt such a thing?"
She continued:

"I stood close as could be to Abe's side, listening to the folk recollect Abe
as a rail-splitter, or the lawyer who recovered a man's horse in court, or the time
he twice threw a wrestling champ. Each added their yarn to the spool. Strung up
all together is a story of a barefooted young man who come along one day driving
a pair a oxen across the prairie, and now he was leaving to be President of the
United States. I'm about well spent Chapman, iffin you don't mind picking up
your story again."

Chapman, Cont'd:

"Granmarm stood by Abe for as long as she could before requesting to
return to our home until Abe was able to join her. Harriet and I gave her our
feather bed. Sure enough Granmarn had little ones twisted all round her once she
was set down to rest. It was late by the time Abe had given each of the neighbors
their time to reminisce."

Mrs. Lincoln knows no quit. Her voice fading, I drew closer as she continued:

"My heart was as big as a steer's just then. Abe again rearranged some of
the young'uns so he could rest his weary head on my shoulder. I done my best to
savor each passing minute but I felt sleep come on a time or two, til I heard the first
chirps of morning coming to life. The day begun and I wasn't to give Abe a sack of
Johnnycake and bacon to tie up to his axe, and I wasn't preferring for this yarn or
that one while we grinned round the fire. Today was for telling my son goodbye. I
was bout as vital as a sack a flour by then. This old lady had done all the pushing
she could muster just to keep up, and I was mostly done for. But it was here now.

"I woke Abe. It was hard on my heart not to let him rest, but I needed my
say with him afore someone come a knocking on the door to take my boy off on
his business. He asked me for the time as I stir him and my heart flung back to
waking him for the fields. Abe was not a boy with a yearning to labor. He use to say
plenty how Tommy taught him how to work the fields, but for sure did not teach
him how to like it. It brung me back to all them days when Abe would beg me off
for more sleep, asking for the time a day so he could make his best case he would
git his chores done even if he slept a while some. So then as was now, when I woke
Abe he asked for the time a day, and I said like I always done when the game was
over, 'Time to get up, Son.' This amused Abe, and he sprung up. We had precious
time now, without a knock yet on the door.

"Told Abe right then how I feared his leaving. Said to my boy he would wrestle with lions and walk across serpents. Then we sung, Rock of Ages. Will you sing it with me now, Billy?"

Mrs. L then reached out her hand to the Writer, who clasped hers in return. Hearing us, Tildy, Dennis, Harriet and Chapman came into the room and added their voices. Mrs. L., still holding Writer's hand, gathered strength for the final verse:

> While I draw this fleeting breath,
> When mine eyes shall close in death,
> When I soar to worlds unknown,
> See Thee on Thy judgment throne,
> Rock of Ages, cleft for me,
> Let me hide myself in Thee.

Mrs. Lincoln took up the story again:

"Just then there come a knock on the door and it was time for him to go. Abe beg them off some, steal us a few more minutes. Time was sparse. I told Abe I prepared this blessing for him:

"May the Lord bid the angels to protect you upon your path. May His face give light to you, show you favor, and bestow upon you wisdom and peace. Lord, act tenderly on my son's behalf and grant his victory over our trials. Merciful Lord, hear my humble request and pardon my selfish ways that it may be Your will that my eyes behold my boy's homecoming afore I should see Thee on Thy judgment throne.

"Just as soon as we said, 'Amen,' I couldn't hold back on it. I told Abe something would befall him and I was plumb afraid I'd never him him again. I know'd it then, that there were people who hated him, who wanted to kill him.

"Abe tried his best to comfort me. His last words were just then, when my son said, 'Trust in the Lord and all will be well. And whatever happens, we will see each other again.'

"All I could muster was to say, 'God bless and keep you, my good son.'

"That was it, Billy. Abe plant his foot on the buggy's sideboard and pull himself up. I seen him turn round for a last look afore the wagon disappeared into a long dark night."

Abe know'd my voice,
straightened up and said,
'Dennis is that you?'
Then invited me in,
and asked Mr. Seward
and the other fellers
to step out a few minutes.

10

Abe Know'd My Voice

Mrs. L finally surrendered herself to exhaustion - lays in her winter stockings beneath several coverlets as darkness filled the windows of both sides of the sagglebag cabin on Goosenest Prairie. She rests along the edge of her feather bed nearest the fire, sure to have it stoked and fed before she settled in.

Tildy and Denny Hanks, Denny's daughter Harriet, and her husband, the previous depositioner, Col. August H. Chapman, and myself divided our small company along the sides of the hearth to allow unobstructed warmth to reach their Granmarm Lincoln.

I undertook to force the subject of value, the family's only contact with the President. "Mr. Hanks, I believe you had the honor of visiting Mr. Lincoln at the Executive Mansion in Washington City, did you not?" He looked at me a moment, and laughing heartily, said: "So that's the yarn you're after is it?" Chuckling to himself for a moment, he winked his eye at Tildy.

Deposition of Dennis Friend Hanks. Elder cousin of the departed President. Present the day of his birth. Widowed husband of Elizabeth Johnston Hanks, aka Betsy. Son-In-Law of Sarah Bush Johnston Lincoln. He began:

"You heard how some Copperhead fellers down at Charleston got into trouble firing on Union soldiers and were sent off to rot in prison, ain't ye? Some smart lawyers down in Charleston tried to get Abe to let them free, but they didn't fetch them worth a cent. So I says to myself, Dennis you're the boy to do it, and I just told the citizens of Charleston so, and they says, 'Hanks, we will give you twelve hundred dollars if you get them fellers released.' You better believe that I took up the offer and waded right in, got my ticket, rode down to Washington and went right up to Uncle Abe's house and asked to see President Lincoln.

"It was during the war, and there were a lot of soldiers around, sticking their blamed guns in everybody's faces. I hunted round for a back door to sneak in, but couldn't find none. A soldier asked me what I was doing there.

"'I want to see Abe Lincoln,' I says.

"'You can't see him now,' he says, like a smarty. Says he, 'There's lots of fellers in talking with him and more that want to get in that come afore you did'. Then I said to him, 'Just show me the hole where the President goes in and out that I'll get to see him.' The feller at the door then said to me, 'Who are you?' I says, 'My name is Hanks, I'm an American citizen, and I want to see Abe Lincoln.' Then the other feller says 'Where are you from?' I says, 'I am from Charleston, Coles County, Illinois.' Then some other feller said, 'That man talks like the President, his voice sounds like his, and maybe he is a relation.'

"'You bet I's kin. Now git!' I says. 'Old Dennis Hanks ain't come clean from Illinois to git his orders from a Jaybird like you!' Te-he-he! That feller got as red as an old turkey gobbler. I waited a minute and nobody done nothing so I just speaks up and says if you'll take me up to his bedroom, I'll have no trouble getting on. I look upon the sights out the window there while I wait for that Jaybird to get his orders figured. I seen Union soldiers camped beneath a half-built Washington Monument, which got this old cobbler thinking, 'Well, don't that beat all?'

"A feller took me up to a door to where Seward was and I looked through a bunch of men and saw Uncle Abe by the stove playing with his little boy and handing him some lemonade or like that and laughing and talking with him. I looked at him a little bit and spoke out in a loud voice, 'Abe what you doing there?' Abe know'd my voice, straightened up and said, 'Dennis is that you?' then invited me in, and asked Mr. Seward and the other fellers to step out a few minutes, said he want to see me privately. So they all went out but me and Uncle Abe. He run and gathered me in like they did in the Bible, so I had to take out my bandanner. Abe looked kind of tired. I reckon they worked him purty hard down there, but he laughed hearty.

"He then ask me how is Mother getting along and all the balance of the family. I just opened up and told Abe my business and let him know that I come to get them fellers in Charleston released. Abe then told me that others been there on the same business, but he had not then thought the men had been punished long enough. So he says now they can go and take care of their families and try to be good men. He pulled out a piece of writing and told me to hand that to Stanton.

"Well I took it to the right fine office of the Secretary of Defense, none other than Edwin M. Stanton. Quicker than a snake through a hollow log, he flew into a passion and says they did too bad a deed to be pardoned. He talked a little bit with me afore he took me with him to see Abe. Mr. Stanton warn't one for hearing these men all have families and they want to go back and care for them and behave themselves, like Abe try to explain, but he just shut up and never said no more nohow.

"Next morning Abe gimme the papers for my case and told me to take them over to Stanton to sign. 'Abe,' says I, 'Blamed if I know where the place is!' Abe laughed and said something about the mountain coming to someone, talking in parables like old times, and sent out a little feller that had on brass buttons enough to stock a store. Purty soon Stanton come rampaging in, snarling about them papers. But Abe made him sign them, and Mr. Stanton went out switching his spike tail coat like a pesky crow.

"I said, 'Abe, if I were as big as you I'd take that little feller across my knees and spank him. He's too sassy.' Abe, he laughed and said Stanton was a bigger feller'n him some ways, and I said he had a darned ugly way of showing it. But that was just like Abe, never running anybody down, finding the good in them, and bearing with their little meannesses. Abe didn't know how to be mean himself. When God made Abe Lincoln He left the meanness out for other folks to divide up among them. I reckon the rest of us got our share.

"Abe told me to look around the city and enjoy myself. 'You go over to the house and Mary'll give you something to eat and a shakedown.' But I put up to a tavern where I could feel more to home. Mary was a good woman, but she was too high-falutin for me. Was home soon enough and launched into a speech a mile long with the news that old base born Denny Hanks seen Uncle Abe and we sprung them Copperhead fellers. Granmarn hung on my every word, feasting on news she could worry herself with. That's all to say for that yarn, I reckon."

I asked Tildy if she would like to offer any general comments. Herein, the deposition of Matilda Johnston Hall:

"I am the youngest stepsister of Abraham Lincoln. I remember coming from Kaintuck. Certainly remember the Ohio River. Went to school about 2 miles or more. Abe was not energetic except in one thing — he was active and persistant in learning. He read everything he could: Robinson Crusoe, The Bible, Watts' hymns. When Father and Mother woud go to Church, they walked about 1½ miles, sometimes rode. When they were gone Abe would take down the Bible, read a verse, give out a hymn, and we would sing — were good singers. Abe was about fifteen years of age. He would preach and we would do the crying. Sometimes he would join in the Chorus of Tears.

"One day my brother, John D. Johnston, caught a land terrapin and brought it to the place where Abe was preaching. There he threw it against the tree crushed the shell and it suffered much, quivered all over. Abe was frightful angry over it, his heart warn't for it. He went on to preach against cruelty to animals, contending that an ant's life is as sweet to it, as our lives are to us.

"Abe would go out to work in the field but somehow end up on a stump speeching. Sometimes he would repeat, almost word-for-word, the sermon he had heard the Sunday before. Call the children and friends around him till Father would come and make him quit, send him to work. Often Abe would make political speeches such as he had heard spoken or seen written. He never forgot anything.

"Once when he was going to the field to work I ran and jumped on his back. Cut my foot on the axe. He said, 'What will we tell Mother as to how this happened?' I said I would tell her I cut my foot on the axe since that will be no lie. Abe said maybe it was so, but it won't be all the truth either, the whole truth. He advised me tell the whole truth and take whatever punishment Mother might deliver.

"Abe seemed to love everybody and every thing. He loved us all and especially Mother. My Mother, I think has given Abe's character. Denny over here is best for speeching if you are inclined to hear any more."

Without pause, the depostition of Dennis Friend Hanks, continued:

"We were all nigh about tickled to death back then when Tom brung a new wife home. She'd been Sally Bush, and Tom'd been in love with her before he met up with Nancy, but her folks wouldn't let Tom have her, because he was shiftless. So she married a man named Johnston and he died. Then her and Tom got married. She had three childern of her own, and a four-horse wagonload of goods that made a heap a difference in a backwoods cabin.

"Yes, Granmarm Lincoln was a woman of property, and could a done better I reckon, but Tom had a kind a way with the women, and maybe it was something she took comfort in to have a man that didn't drink and cuss none. She made a heap more a Tom, too, more than poor Nancy did. There were eight of us then to do fur, but Granmarm had faculty and didn't appear to be hurried or worried none. Little Sairy just chirked right up with a mother and two sisters for comp'ny. Abe used to say he was glad Sairy had some good times. She married purty young and died with her fust baby. I reckon it was like Nancy, she didn't have no sort of care.

"We were all purty ragged and dirty when Granmarm Lincoln got there. The fust thing she did was to tell me to tote one of Tom's carpenter benches to a place outside the door, near the horse trough. Then she had me and Abe and John D. Johnston, her boy, fill the trough with spring water. She put out a big gourd full of soft soap, and another one to dip water with, and told us boys to wash up for dinner. You just naturally had to be somebody when Granmarm was around. Then—te-he-he-he! She set some kind of a dead-fall trap for Tommy and got him to join the Baptist Church! Cracky, she was some punkins!

"She didn't have no education herself, but she know'd what learning could do for folks. Granmarm always put a candle on the mantelpiece for Abe, if she had one. And as like as not Abe'd eat his supper there, taking anything she'd give him that he could gnaw at and read at the same time. She never let the childern pester him. She always said Abe was going to be a great man someday, and she wasn't going to have him hindered."

"When Abe was nineteen he was as tall as he was ever going to be, I reckon. He was the ganglin'est, awkwardest feller that ever stepped over a ten-rail snake fence. He had to duck to git through a door and appeared to be all joints. Tom used to say Abe looked as if he'd been chopped out with an ax and needed a jack plane took to him. Granmarm often told Abe that his feet being clean didn't matter so much, because she could scour the floor, but he'd better wash his head, or he'd be a rubbing dirt off on her nice whitewashed rafters. That put an idea in his head, I reckon. Several of us older ones were married then, and there was always a passel of youngsters round the place. One day Abe put them up to wading in the mud puddle by the horse trough. Then he took them one by one, turned them upside down, and walked them across the ceiling, them a screaming fit to kill.

"Granmarm come in, and it was so blamed funny she set down and laughed, though she said Abe'd oughter to be spanked. I don't know how far he had to go for more lyme, but he whitewashed the ceiling all over again. Granmarm said many a time that Abe'd never made her a mite of trouble, or spoke a cross word to her since she come into the house. He was the best boy she ever seen.

"Abe had a powerful good memory. He'd go to church and come home and say over the sermon as good as the preacher. He'd often do it for Granmarm, when she couldn't go, and she said it was just as good as going herself. He'd say over everything from beloved brethern to Amen without cracking a smile, pass a pewter plate for a collection and then we'd all join him in singing the Doxology.

Granmarm thought a heap of Abe, and he did of her, and I reckon they'd a done most anything for one another.

"She seemed to know Abe had more pride than the rest of us. He always had a extra pair of buttenut dyed jeans pants, and a white shirt. When he was only thirteen Granmarm Lincoln said to him: 'Abe, you git holt of some muslin somewheres and have some white shirts, so you can go to folk's houses right.' So he cut nine cords of wood and got nine yards of unbleached muslin, and she bleached it and shrunk it and made him two shirts. He put one of them on every Sunday. Maybe Abe wouldn't a been the man he was if it hadn't been for his mother and stepmother encouraging him."

Dennis Hanks shifted uneasily in his chair. He stared at the flickering shadows of the firelight on the wall, in dazed horror, as at some fearful whispered fate. He spoke:

"I kain't believe it yet. I was setting in my shop pegging away at a shoe, when a man come running in from the street, looking like a ghost, and said, 'Dennis, honest Abe's dead - shot dead!'

"It was in April, and the sun was shining and the grass turning green, just as if nothing had happened, and it seemed to me like the earth had stopped. There wasn't any trading done scarcely, and people standing round in the streets crying. I had to go out to the farm to tell Granmarm. Tom'd been dead a good while, and she was living out here on Goosenest Prairie, alone.

"'Granmarm,' says I, "Abe's dead."

"'Yes, I know, Denny. I know'd they'd kill him. I been a waiting for it,' and she never asked no questions. She was gittin purty old, and I reckon she thought she'd soon join him. She never counted on seeing him again after he went down to Washington City nohow. He come out to the farm to see her, and when he kissed her goodbye she reached her old hands up to his shoulders and looked at him as if he's a laying in his coffin then, and says to him: 'You'll never come back, Abraham!'"

"Don't you worry, Mama," he says. "I'll come back all right."

"Well, I myself, nothing but a little dried up nubbin of a shoemaker. Appears to me like there ain't been nothing happened worth talking about, and nobody much worth talking to since Abe's gone.

"Some folks think you won't know anybody when you git to heaven, but I bet I'll know Abe Lincoln. He went straight there, and I ain't taking no chances on it, but am living the best I know how, by church rules, so I can go to heaven too, and meet up with Abe. There was a preacher feller come here once, and I was talking to him about there not being any sense in Abe being shot thataway, and him only fifty-six and strong as a horse. And he said that he reckoned Abe'd done his work and the Lord know'd best.

"'Done his work, hey?' I hollered. 'He hadn't lived his life. I wouldn't a give a darn if he'd never done another lick of work, if he'd just come home and let me visit with him once in a while.'

"There won't be another man like Abe Lincoln this side of Judgement Day!"

"Amen Son," Mrs. Sarah Bush Lincoln spoke.

When I was about to leave she arose — took me by the hand — wept — and bade me goodbye — Saying I shall never see you again — and if you see Mrs. Abm Lincoln and family tell them I send them my best and tenderest love — Goodbye my good son's friend — farewell.

September 8, 1865
Charleston Depot
Charleston, Illinois

Dearest Anna,

In haste I write, as my free thoughts
naturally turn upon you, my love.

I awoke this morning as full of gratitude as
I could possibly be, for the many gifts given
to me by Mr. Lincoln. Alas, even in his
passage, he gives me more immeasurable joy —
today with the introduction of his stepmother.
I interviewed her in person, and took notes of
her conversation. She rose in mind high above
her surroundings, she was a true woman. The
information thus given me by the good old
lady, the kind and loving mother, God bless
her, put me on nettles, as it were, and so we
commenced our afternoon together. Mr. Lincoln
for years supported or helped to support his aged
father and mother; it is to ~~the~~ the honor of
Mr. L. that he dearly loved his stepmother,
and it is equally true that she idolized her
stepson. So timely was her arrival, so tender
her love, to make him a person again, a man
of the mud, flowers and mind that were his
native West.

On to Indiana. By your sweet side, in
the comfort of your love, I yearn to be.

Your husband,

William H. Herndon, Billy

Their Humble
But Worthy Home

~~~

The Plains whistled and whispered through nights cooler than days on Goosenest Prairie. Here in her bedside nearest the warm glow of fire rested Abraham Lincoln's stepmother, Sarah Bush Johnston Lincoln; Known to some as Granmarm, Granmarm Lincoln, Sally, Sarah, Sairy, Aunt Sairy, Daughter Sarah Bush, Daughter Sarah, Sis or Mama. Here the once proud body of Elizabethtown, Kentucky relived the joys and sorrows in her dreams. So proceeded the process of departure from the living earth still lingering. Sometimes a girl of the stalwart stock that crowded the Bush family cabin back in Kaintuck, other times she might see Tommy again.

Ah the sweet slumber when her mind drifted backwards to a memory of her boy. Not of her, because of her. He could laugh her awake with the things he said and did, or just appearing so protruding generally. He could cry her awake too, until the day came. Abe & his Father are in Heaven she had no doubt, and she wanted to go there — go where they are — God bless Abraham.

LINCOLN

THOMAS *and* SARAH BUSH LINCOLN
1778-1851   1788-1869

FATHER AND STEPMOTHER
OF OUR MARTYRED PRESIDENT

THEIR HUMBLE BUT WORTHY HOME
GAVE THE WORLD
ABRAHAM LINCOLN

Photographs

Sarah Bush Johnston Lincoln

William H. Herndon

Thomas Lincoln

The Saddlebag Cabin on Goosenest Prairie

Primary Resources

The Boyhood of Lincoln, Eleanor Atkinson
Lincoln in New Orleans, Richard Campanella
Abraham Lincoln and Coles County, Illinois, Charles H. Coleman
Lincoln's Herndon, David Herbert Donald
Life of Lincoln, William H. Herndon
The Hidden Lincoln, Emanuel Hertz
Lincoln's Preparation for Greatness, Sen. Paul Simon
He Knew Lincoln: And Other Billy Brown Stories, Ida Minerva Tarbell
Lincoln's Mothers, Dorothy Clarke Wilson
Herndon's Informants, Douglas L. Wilson and Rodney O. Davis
Lincoln's Youth, Louis A. Warren
The Story of Young Abraham Lincoln, Wayne Whipple

Acknowledgments

My life pretty much begins and ends with my two favorite people to hang out with, my Wife and Daughter. My Mom and Dad have encouraged me long past reason... My Niece and Nephew, yeah, that's my family alright. It's nice to know you... From my Aunt Sue I did not have to look far for an example of a Stepmother whose love could not be confined by bloodlines. To these Stepmoms and Stepdads, I am humbled by the opportunity to honor you... For the experience to draw on conversing with a slightly oyscavet (loosely translated as pleasantly confused), endearing, ornery, hilarious, and always cold, elderly person, I have Papa Jerry... Thankfully, Rep. Patrick Murphy (of PA) and Alan Sheriff were supportive in the beginning. I recall my father's story of the advisor who encouraged him to pursue med school, long past reason (a family trait?). What if, he later wondered, he picked a lesser advisor? ...Along the way I went to Charleston, IL, where I met Nancy Easter-Schick, a blood-relative to Abraham Lincoln, and in so many ways the living embodiment of his beloved stepmother... For inspiration, my fellow author-in-arms, and lord of the sloppy dice, there is Robby W... With Charlene Keel (charlenekeel.com) came healthy connectivity and narrative, a mom's tenderness, and excellent adventures. The Jenkins Group proved a deep well of professional guidance... My day with the Louis A. Warren Collection, thanks to Jane Gastineau of the Lincoln Financial Foundation Collection at the Indiana State Museum... Rosemary Knower loves to tell it the way it is, making her a great editor. ...The irrepressible force for good, Ellyn Phillips, and the entire ALS Association of Philadelphia is worthy of the most worthy adversary... To Anne and Craig, Gene, Debra Sue, and Carole King, the sages wasting their valuable time helping me when I was really in the wilderness... The super sleuth Lilly, keeping things honest. Jodi and Deb, who really didn't help at all, but we can't stop loving you anyway... Big Joel, crossing dirt to Springfield, IL and back. ...And finally to the caregivers: Phyllis, Krystle, Erika, Liz, Tina, Patty, Amy, Beth, and Kathy, who provide our entire family with such comfort.

It has been my great pleasure to take my turn at the challenge of revealing the reticent A. Lincoln.

Cover and interior design created by BadCat Design.

Jeff Oppenheimer

William H. Herndon's Notes

September 8, 1865

⌒

Friday — Old Mrs. Lincolns Home — 8m South of Charleston — Septr 8th 1865

When I first reachd the House of Mrs. Lincoln and were introduced to her by Col A H. Chapman her grandson by marriage — I did not Expect to get much out of her — She seemed to old & feeble — : She asked me my name 2 or 3 times and where I lived as often — and woud say — "Where Mr. Lincoln lived once his friend too" She breathed badly at first but She seemed to be struggling at last to arouse her self — or to fix her mind on the subject. Gradually by introducing simple questions to her — about her age — marriage — Kentucky — Thomas Lincoln — her former husband Johnston her children — grand children She awoke — as it were a new being — her Eyes were clear & calm: her flesh is white & pure — not Coarse or material — is tall — has bluish large gray Eyes

Mrs. Thomas Lincoln Says —

I knew Mr. Lincoln in Ky — I married Mr. Johnson — he died about 1817 or 18 — Mr. Lincoln came back to Ky, having lost his wife — Mr. Thos Lincoln & Myself were married in 1819 — left Ky — went to Indiana — moved there in a team — think Krume movd us. Her is our old Bible dated 1819 [1]: it has Abes name in it. Here is Barclay's dictionary dated 1799 [2] — : it has Abe's name in it, though in a better hand writing — both are boyish scrawls — When we landed in Indiana Mr. Lincoln had erected a good log cabin — tolerably Comfortable. This is the bureau I took to Indiana in 1819 — cost $45 in Ky Abe were then young — so were his Sister. I dressed Abe & his sister up — looked more human. Abe slept up stairs — went up on pins stuck in the logs — like a ladder — Our bed steds were original creations — none such now — made of poles & Clapboards — Abe were about 9 ys of age when I landed in Indiana — The country were wild — and desolate. Abe were a good boy: he didn't like physical labor — were diligent for Knowledge — wished to Know & if pains & Labor would get it he were sure to get it. He were the best boy I ever saw. He read all the books he could lay his hands on — I can't remember dates nor names — am about 75 ys of age — Abe read the bible some, though not as much as said: he sought more congenial books — suitable for his age. I think newspapers were had in Indiana as Early as 1824 & up to 1830 when we moved to Ills — Abe were a Constant reader of them — I am sure of this for the years of 1827 — 28 — 29 — 30. The name of the Louisville Journal [3] seems to sound like one. Abe read histories, papers — & other books — cant name any one — have forgotten. Abe had no particular religion — didnt think of that question at that time, if he ever did — He never talked about it. He read diligently — studied in the day time — didnt after night much — went to bed Early — got up Early & then read — Eat his breakfast — go to work in the field with the men. Abe read all the books he could lay his hands on — and when he came across a passage that Struck him he would write it down on boards if he had no paper & keep it there till he did get paper — then he would re-write it — look at it repeat it — He had a copy book — a kind of scrap book in which he put down all things and this preserved them. He ciphered on boards when he had no paper or no slate and when the board would get too black he would shave it off with a drawing knife and go on again: When he had paper he put his sums down on it. [4] His copy book is here now or were lately (Here it were shown me by Mr. Thos Johnson) Abe, when old folks were at our house, were a silent & attentive observer — never speaking or asking questions till they were gone and then he must understand Every thing — even to the smallest thing — Minutely & Exactly — : he would then repeat it over to himself again & again — sometimes in one form and then in another & when it were fixed in his mind to suit him he became Easy and he never lost that fact or his understanding of it. Sometimes he seemed pestered to give Expression to his ideas and got mad almost at one who couldn't Explain plainly what he wanted to convey. He would hear sermons preached — come home — take the children out — get on a stump or log and almost repeat it word for word — He made other Speeches — Such as interested him and the children. His father had to make him quit sometimes as he quit his own work to speak & made the other children as well as the men quit their work. As a usual thing Mr. Lincoln never made Abe quit reading to do anything if he could avoid it. He would do it himself first. Mr. Lincoln could read a little & could scarcely write his name: hence he wanted, as he himself felt the uses & necessities of Education his boy Abraham to learn & he Encouraged him to do it in all ways he could — Abe were a poor boy, & I can say what scarcely one woman — a mother — can say in a thousand and it is this — Abe never gave me a cross word or look and never refused in fact, or Even in appearance, to do any thing I requested him. I never gave him a cross word in all my life. He were Kind to Every body and to Every thing and always accommodate others if he could — would do so willingly if he could.

His mind & mine — what little I had seemed to run together — move in the same channel — Abe could Easily learn & long remember and when he did learn anything he learned it well and thoroughly. What he thus learned he stowed away in his memory which were Extremely good — What he learned and Stowed away were well defined in his own mind — repeated over & over again & again till it were so defined and fixed firmly & permanently in his Memory. He rose Early — went to bed Early, not reading much after night. Abe were a moderate Eater and I now have no remembrance of his Special dish: he Sat down & ate what were set before him, making no complaint: he seemd Careless about this. I cooked his meals for nearly 15 years — . He always had good health — never were sick — were very careful of his person — were tolerably neat and clean only — Cared nothing for clothes — so that they were clean & neat — fashion cut no figure with him — nor Color — nor Stuff nor material — were Careless about these things. He were more fleshy in Indiana than Ever in Ills — . I saw him Every year or two — He were here — after he were Elected President of the US. (Here the old lady stopped — turned around & cried — wiped her Eyes — and proceeded) As Company would Come to our house Abe were a silent listener — wouldn't speak — would sometimes take a book and retire aloft — go to the stable or field or woods — and read — . Abe were always fond of fun — sport — wit & jokes — He were sometimes very witty indeed. He never drank whiskey or other strong drink — were temperate in all things — too much so I thought sometimes — He never told me a lie in his life — never Evaded — never Equivocated never dodged — nor turned a Corner to avoid any chastisement or other responsibility. He never swore or used profane language in my presence nor in others that I now remember of — He duly reverenced old age — loved those best about his own age — played with those under his age — he listened to the aged — argued with his Equals — but played with the children — . He loved animals genery and treated them Kindly: he loved children well very well — . There seemed to be nothing unusual in his love for animals or his own Kind — though he treated Every body & Every thing Kindly — humanely — Abe didnt Care much for crowds of people: he choose his own Company which were always good. He were not very fond of girls as he seemed to me. He sometimes attended Church. He would repeat the sermon over again to the children. The sight of such a thing amused all and did Especially tickle the Children. When Abe were reading My husband took particular Care not to disturb him — would let him read on and on till Abe quit of his own accord. He were dutiful to me always — he loved me truly I think. I had a son John who were raised with Abe Both were good boys, but I must Say — both now being dead that Abe were the best boy I Ever Saw or Ever Expect to see. I wish I had died when my husband died. I did not want Abe to run for Presdt — did not want him Elected — were afraid Somehow or other — felt it in my heart that Something would happen him and when he came down to see me after he were Elected Presdt I still felt that Something told me that Something would befall Abe and that I should see him no more. Abe & his father are in Heaven I have no doubt, and I want to go there — go where they are — God bless Abm

Ate dinner with her — sat on my west side — left arm — ate a good hearty dinner she did —

When I were about to leave she arose — took me by the hand — wept — and bade me goodby — Saying I shall never see you again — and if you see Mrs. Abm Lincoln & family tell them I send them my best & tenderest love — Goodby my good son's friend — farewell.